Medicine in the Making of Modern Britain, 1700–1920

HISTORICAL CONNECTIONS

Series editors
Tom Scott, University of Liverpool
Geoffrey Crossick, University of Essex
John Davis, University of Connecticut
Joanna Innes, Somerville College, University of Oxford

Medicine in the Making of Modern Britain, 1700–1920

Christopher Lawrence

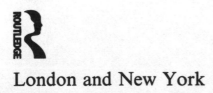

London and New York

First published 1994
by Routledge
11 New Fetter Lane, London EC4P 4EE

Simultaneously published in the USA and Canada
by Routledge
29 West 35th Street, New York, NY 10001

© 1994 Christopher Lawrence

Typeset in Monotype Times New Roman
by the EPPP Group at Routledge
Printed and bound in Great Britain
by Mackays of Chatham plc, Chatham, Kent

British Library Cataloguing in Publication Data
A catalogue record for this book is available from the
British Library

Library of Congress Cataloging in Publication Data
A catalog record for this book is available from the
Library of Congress

ISBN 0-415-09168-3

To Peter Hopkins and Willie Sandison
who taught me more than they knew.

Contents

Series editors' preface

Historical Connections is a new series of short books on important historical topics and debates, written primarily for those studying and teaching history. The books will offer original and challenging works of synthesis that will make new themes accessible, or old themes accessible in new ways, build bridges between different chronological periods and different historical debates, and encourage comparative discussion in history.

If the study of history is to remain exciting and creative, then the tendency to fragmentation must be resisted. The inflexibility of older assumptions about the relationship between economic, social, cultural and political history has been exposed by recent historical writing, but the impression has sometimes been left that history is little more than a chapter of accidents. This series will insist on the importance of processes of historical change, and it will explore the connections within history: connections between different layers and forms of historical experience, as well as connections that resist the fragmentary consequences of new forms of specialism in historical research.

Historical Connections will put the search for these connections back at the top of the agenda by exploring new ways of uniting the different strands of historical experience, and by affirming the importance of studying change and movement in history.

Geoffrey Crossick
John Davis
Joanna Innes
Tom Scott

Acknowledgements

Michael Neve and David Blackbourn first interested me in and encouraged me to write this book. I have found much friendship in the great care a number of people took when reading and commenting on an earlier draft. Many thanks to Mike Barfoot, Bill Bynum, Dan Fox, Chris Hamlin, Stephen Jacyna, Victoria Lawrence, Mike Neve, Kathy Panama, Roy Porter, Steve Sturdy and Andrew Wear. Thanks too to the publishers and the series editors for their enthusiasm and particularly Joanna Innes for her helpful comments. For her patience at the W.P. many thanks also to Lyn Dobson.

Christopher Lawrence
London, August 1993

Introduction

I qualified in medicine in 1970. For two or three decades before that, medicine in Britain was, arguably, on an historical peak. In the hospital the consultant was held in awe by the patient and was an undisputed authority for juniors, nurses and students. Outside of it he (most consultants were men) was perceived as an exemplary member of the community. The surgeon in particular was held in high esteem. Heroic was an epithet that scarcely seemed out of place in the aftermath of the first heart transplant operation, performed by Christiaan Barnard in December 1967. In the localities in which they worked general practitioners had the image of trusted family advisors, avuncular, moral confidantes. 'Go and talk to your doctor' was every agony aunt's stock reply when the correspondent's question bordered on the technical. Middle class and respectable, the medical profession as a whole seemed a body to whom matters of health, sickness and morality could be entrusted. Diagnostically and therapeutically, clinical medicine was perceived to have been the beneficiary of extensive scientific research. Molecular biology was being hailed as a saviour of mankind. Wonder was the word frequently coupled with drugs. New technologies – heart–lung machinery, diagnostic ultrasound – were presented as tangible evidence of progress. It was not hard to find the word 'miracle' conjoined to medicine. Organizationally too, medicine was a source of satisfaction. In the National Health Service (NHS), the British proudly proclaimed that they had created the finest provision for medical care in the world.

Of course there were complaints and criticisms in those decades. Some of the latter were far from superficial and they drew on a long tradition which questioned the values incorporated within medical knowledge and practice. Nevertheless since the 1970s medicine has been rapidly descending the other side of the peak. Nowadays for every sensational story about the transplantation of a baboon's liver into a baby, there is a serious article wondering whether this is medicine out of control; whether treatment is being pursued solely on the grounds that technical intervention is possible, or because no patient should be denied any treatment available. Likewise today, for every television programme praising the dedication and service to be found in the great hospitals, there is another, questioning whether or not these institutions are the beneficiaries of a gross misallocation of resources; whether the disadvantages of poverty, age and disablement are getting their fair share of dedication. Should the provision of good housing or a clean and safe environment come second to the delivery of acute medical care? More broadly, is clinical medicine the best means to national health? Similarly, for each million put into scientific research there is now a sceptic who queries whether this is the way to solve problems about human values. Should we pay such a price for a projected future good? Do we need a knowledge-producing machine of these dimensions? Is it even the *sort* of knowledge we need? Finally, these days, the affirmation by doctors that clinical freedom should be sacred, evokes the response that this claim protects professional interests while expropriating from people the right to make moral choices. What is this 'clinical freedom' that cannot be tainted with 'political' inference?

There is no timeless thing, medicine, which is intrinsically or essentially good or bad. Medicine, what we value in it and why are related, historically contingent matters and thus open to historical analysis. There is no necessary reason why a medicine that can transplant hearts should be admired. Such a state of affairs must provoke the historian to ask the question, how did such a medicine become an object of admiration? To answer this question we need to dig very deep into the general social and cultural fabric. Here I explore the historical making of the medicine that was, and to a great extent still is, so important to us. Politicians and many writers of popular and serious histories often depict the Second World War as a watershed in the medical past. They see the inauguration of the NHS in 1948 as a profound break and regard the technology, science, practice and organization of post-war medicine as radically different from what went before. I argue, however, that the principal features of post-war medicine were actually elaborations of social and cultural formations which had been made over the previous two centuries and were in place by the 1920s. In 1919 the Ministry of Health was created and this occasion forms a convenient end-point for my more detailed argument. It is not that there have been no major changes since 1920. There has been large-scale reorganization and the relation of this to the historical transformations described here I sketch in at the end. There have also been changes in the social estimation of medicine. One of the minor cultural threads which characterized British life 1920–1970 was the increasing public endorsement of modern medicine. Only aspects of that endorsement have been studied (Fox and Lawrence 1988).

By the end of the second decade of the twentieth century, many of the complex ideas, assumptions and practices which constitute modern medicine had been created. Here I offer an historical explanation of why these things had the form they did. For a long time medical historians writing about Britain have understood the years roughly corresponding to the industrial revolution as an age when relatively modern concepts of the body and disease were created. More recent studies have shown how, in the eighteenth century, medical categories were increasingly drawn on to account for a changing, commercializing society. Even more recently the period 1880–1920 has assumed considerable significance when viewed from the perspective of the organization of medical work. All three of these themes will be pursued here: changing ideas about the body and disease, the increasing use of medical categories as general explanatory resources and the organization of medical work. I will not, however, employ these analytical approaches separately and limit them to the periods to which they have been most fruitfully applied so far. Rather I hope to demonstrate their relevance to understanding the whole period I examine and their essential relatedness.

My aim is to show how, in the two centuries covered here, the clinical encounter was made into a transaction of great social and cultural importance in Britain. By the 1920s, treatment in hospital, especially of the acutely ill young, using scientifically informed, potent therapy, had become the object of much admiration. It was valued, simultaneously, as a means to address individual suffering and as a major instrument of social betterment. This medicine was predicated on a view of disease as a biological process, best comprehended in the laboratory and best dealt with by technical intervention. It regarded sickness, by contrast, largely as a consequence of self-neglect. This was not a medicine well equipped with resources for giving meaning to suffering it could not alleviate, providing care and technical assistance for the disadvantaged and chronically sick, seeking the wider determinants of disease or understanding health in terms other than the physiological. Nevertheless, the interventive clinical encounter was given a key position in welfare policy. Clinical medicine was celebrated as a powerful tool for ameliorating the human lot, promoting social progress and, ultimately, creating wealth. Crucial to this account of medicine, and deeply embedded in late nineteenth-century political change, was the view that access to professional clinical care should be a citizen's right. It is this nexus of assumptions, views and practices I seek to explicate, for they are at the heart of the current medical crisis.

The perception that many of the major formations of modern medicine were in place by 1920 is by no means my own. Indeed much excellent twentieth-century medical historiography has taken the conclusion as its starting point (Fox 1986a; Lewis 1992). Rich though the literature on the history of medicine in the eighteenth and nineteenth centuries has become in the last few years, what we do not have is a synthetic account of the ways in which clinical medicine, in all its aspects, became an important part of the fabric of late nineteenth- and early twentieth-century life.[1] This, I hope, is what I have done. As the reader will soon discover, this book is an argument and not an attempted synthesis of the best work. It is not a history of medicine and I make no apology for the absence of various subjects which, tremendously important though they are, are subservient to my theme: demography, epidemiology, nursing and midwifery, for example. Most important, this is a work primarily about British culture and society, not simply about medicine. In support of this claim, I suggest my analysis fits not only medicine, but accords with accounts of other areas of British life in the twentieth century. In industry, the family, in morals and the market, the last two decades mark a questioning of social and cultural patterns which had been established by the 1920s. Most obviously what characterizes this questioning is a certain distrust of all those things which once seemed so obviously to offer the way forward, notably planning, technical expertise and professionalism. If there was a rise of professional society in the late nineteenth century we may be witnessing its decline (Perkin 1989).

Central to the way I argue this book will be the active voice. The social and cultural changes which I discuss did not simply happen. At the detailed level they were made by the medical profession as that profession made itself. Part of that making, I will argue, was the profession's success in bounding itself. By bounding I mean that, by the 1920s, the profession to a great extent controlled the production of medical knowledge and the organization of most medical practice and related occupations. It also controlled many of the meanings that could be given to sickness. One indication of this today is the way in which alternative medicine, overwhelmingly, employs the anatomical, physiological and pathological categories of orthodox medicine. What alternative medical systems offer are so-called holistic understanding and alternative therapeutics.[2] The preference, in some quarters, for the term 'complementary' instead of 'alternative', makes this point. If outside interference in medicine has become increasingly marginal this century, professional medical involvement in British culture and society since the mid-nineteenth century has been monumental. None of the changes I describe happened in isolation; they were paralleled by and related to similar changes in other occupations and consequent on more profound changes in British society, notably the rise of industrial capitalism. Although my analysis is confined to Britain, a similar case could be made for North America and much of Europe. The details would differ considerably but the broad story would be much the same. Indeed, because of medicine's claims to privileged knowledge of health and disease, the history would be odd if it did not look similar to that in other industrial societies.

For stylistic reasons I will refer to regular practitioners of all sorts as doctors, even though for much of the period under consideration they were not accorded that courtesy title. Since, until recently, most doctors were men, I will stick with masculine pronouns. Since most doctors usually wrote about the sick as if they too were men, the masculine will be more correct in that context.[3] By clinic or clinical I mean a doctor–patient interaction, either diagnostic or therapeutic or preventative, but not in any particular institutional setting.

1 The Enlightenment

If medicine in twentieth-century Britain consists of a constellation of occupations and meanings mainly clustered around the medical profession, if medicine has, as I have suggested, become bounded, in the eighteenth century this was much less the case. Then, the word medicine did not point preponderantly to a single profession, to a particular view of disease or to a particular sort of institution. Although a great deal of medical boundary making was done by some groups, increasingly done as the century wore on, for the most part such attempts at enclosure were of no consequence to the majority of the population and were ignored. Treating and caring for the sick were no one's monopoly. There were certainly plenty of sick people to be cared for. Epidemic diseases, such as smallpox and measles, and endemic ones, such as the ubiquitous 'fever', were part of everyone's experience. Crippling chronic diseases, consumption and rickets for example, were common, and the price, very often, of long hard labour, poverty and an economy at the mercy of nature.

If the practice of medicine in the eighteenth century was not closed when compared to today, either socially (as an occupation) or culturally (in the meanings given to sickness), this does not mean that we cannot discern any order or assumptions in the treatment of the sick. Quite the reverse: the order was that of a parochial, patronage-based but increasingly commercial society. Matters such as provision for education, the protection of the helpless and the care of the sick were regarded as the responsibility of individuals (or groups of them voluntarily united), the family or, at most, the parish. Although central directives (as in the Poor Law, for instance) ultimately determined the handling of many of these things, other than in exceptional circumstances such matters were not, and were not considered to be, the day-to-day concern of the state. As regards the assumptions which informed healing, these were various, but concerns about place and providence figured large.

At the disposal of the sick in the eighteenth century were many healing resources but access to them was not unrestricted. For most people choice was limited by such obvious factors as geography. The sorts of healer within reach depended on which of the nations of the kingdom you lived in and whether you spent your life in a city, a town or in the country. Choice was channelled by cultural factors: regional, local and familial traditions; religious and political beliefs; and your sense of your station in society. Having money made the widest range of choices available.

Among the very poor, the family or a neighbour might be the first and last resort in sickness. Very often someone locally might be known to be skilful in the use of herbs or in bonesetting; when they were not going about their usual business, delivering babies perhaps, or shoeing horses. Among religious sects such as the Methodists, someone with recognized healing skills might take responsibility for the sick. In relatively closed communities, the forces of patronage would often come into play: the parson or the squire's wife, for example, might treat the sick farm labourer, his wife or his children (Porter, R. 1985c). The act of treating sickness is loaded with cultural concerns; it can be used to carry all sorts of meanings which bear little obvious relation to medicine narrowly defined. In eighteenth-century Britain it worked on a day-to-day basis (and still does) to strengthen (and sometimes weaken) both particular social relations and the general sense of whether society was properly ordered. Whether or not it was viewed as therapeutically effective, healing could be used to reinforce or repudiate the religious and political ideas which explained and justified the way things were. In an act of healing, the poor, for example, might learn, among other things, the value or otherwise of neighbourliness or that they should be grateful to those in a higher station.

A wide variety of healing practices existed in the eighteenth century. Although in general it was fashionable in literary society to express faith in Enlightenment, in rational medicine and in progress, among the poor (but not only the poor), magical, folkloric and religious healing remained common (Fissell 1991). In the seventeenth century, invocation of magical powers added a significant ideological dimension to the political struggles of the Civil War. Many of those who invoked, or were thought to have invoked, such powers were ruthlessly suppressed. In the eighteenth century, magical healing practices were widespread but existing predominantly among the poor they offered little or no political threat. Nothing in the eighteenth century, however, was unalloyed. Magically derived remedies might easily rub shoulders in the kitchen of the manor house with cures from other traditions, the tried and tested herbs for instance. The poor, too, might encounter regular or orthodox medicine from the parson or the squire's wife who had read a popular exposition of it, quite possibly in the work of the physician, William Buchan, whose *Domestic Medicine* was first published in 1769 (Lawrence, C. 1975; Rosenberg 1983). The poor, on occasion, might even receive treatment from a regular practitioner, most likely an apothecary or a so-called surgeon. After all one of the purposes of local rates, levied on property owners, was to provide assistance for the parish poor in times of distress. In some parishes, at some times, this might extend to paying a practitioner (not necessarily belonging to one of the regular orders) to attend the sick. In particular a surgeon might be required to intervene at a difficult childbirth. Midwifery was generally women's business and the ceremony which surrounded birth designated it a rite of passage, not a medical event. Still, if a child died, or got stuck in the pelvis, the parish might pay for a surgeon who, it was hoped, could skilfully use crushing and extracting implements to save a woman's life (Wilson 1985a, 1985b).

Who, then, were these orthodox or regular practitioners and what, if anything, did they have in common with other sorts of healer? To answer the latter part first, the thing all healers had in common was that, at least until late in the eighteenth century, they practised only individual, usually face-to-face medicine.[1] It was almost always for a fee, generally paid by the patient or perhaps the patient's family or friends. Except for the work of military and naval surgeons, practice was usually beyond the everyday concerns of the state. Which is not to say, once again, that it had nothing to do with the ordering and working of eighteenth-century society.

Orthodox medicine had three orders of practitioners – physicians, surgeons and apothecaries. In terms of self-estimation and, usually, of economic reward, physicians comprised the élite. To call them members of a profession is to introduce a word whose meaning changed quite drastically in the nineteenth century, yet it is meaningful if we use it, as they did, to designate themselves as qualified to practise 'physic' – that branch of the healing art concerned with internal medicine. Physicians were avid, but relatively unsuccessful, boundary builders. In London they sealed themselves off in their Royal College which had been founded in the sixteenth century. That they had a Royal College at all is significant, for it amounted to an endorsement by the ruling class of a particular form of medical culture. What that medical culture was can be seen in the qualifications the College insisted on for membership and the sort of medicine that it required its members to practise. The College preferred its members to have an MD granted by a recognized university and it only admitted Oxford and Cambridge graduates to its inner circle, the Fellowship. The physician then, like men of the law or the church, was book-learned. This learning extended to more than knowledge of internal medicine. Physicians regarded themselves as learned in all aspects of the healing art. This knowledge, said the physician, gave him (there were no women physicians) the right to oversee all of medicine. The physician considered practitioners of the two other branches of healing, surgery and dispensing, as his manual attendants. In their ideal ordering of medicine, physicians built a structure that valued mind over matter, head over hand, art over artisan, gentility over labour.

The College attempted to control the practice of physic in London, and to some extent throughout England and Wales, by a system of licensing. It also attempted, indirectly, to regulate the work of surgeons and the dispensers (apothecaries). It had some success in controlling practitioners who called themselves physicians, but was hopelessly unsuccessful in regulating the practice of physic. Anybody and everybody practised internal medicine. Why, then, did the wealthy pay a great deal to hire a man who was called by himself, and others, a physician, when they could just as easily call in a lay practitioner who might well be less expensive? The answer lies in those complexities of patronage that made eighteenth-century society work. Just as portrait painting, authorship and furniture making, for example, were entwined in the patronage network, so too was medicine.

Physicians considered themselves the healers of the well-to-do, and thus they cultivated the learning and manners of the orders they aspired to attend. In the physician's ideal self-portrait he was university educated and widely read in the most modern and ancient literature. In practice the physician's task was to draw on this modern and classical knowledge and reason out what was occurring beneath the sufferer's skin. His learning told him, in general, what were the possible origins of the sick person's symptoms in the darkness of the body. His capacity to reason, to apply his knowledge, allowed him to proceed in a particular case from the obvious sensory data to hidden causes. Apart from feeling the pulse the physician rarely touched the patient during a consultation. Propriety (contact between a gentleman physician and genteel sufferers) discouraged it and the structure of medical reasoning rendered it unnecessary. As we shall see, propriety and reasoning, were intimately related.

In his practice the eighteenth-century physician reasoned about sickness in ways quite unlike our own. Physicians recognized apparently distinct diseases, the names for many of which were quite ancient:

pneumonia, arthritis, phthisis, pleurisy, whooping cough. They knew from their book-learning the possible symptoms of these diseases and also the hidden disorders (the pathology) which could give rise to the symptoms. These hidden disorders comprised a great number of imbalances in the relationship between the solid fibres and the many fluids which were held to constitute the body.

But it was at this point that medicine began rather than ended. For us, putting a name to a group of symptoms and signs, diagnosis, is to give disease a specific identity at one or several levels – anatomical, biochemical, genetic, for example – it implicates a specific determining cause.[2] The name often points to a possible, possibly immediate, cure. For the eighteenth-century physician, giving a name to a patient's disorder did not define it anywhere nearly so comprehensively. For physicians and sufferers alike, a sick person's condition was seen to follow from a combination of errors of various sorts, many of which were held to be the consequence of self-neglect. Faults in constitution, inheritance, diet, bowel habits, sexual activities, exercise, sleeping patterns and so forth were described as combining to produce disease. Although this disease might have a name – pneumonia, for example – what mattered were the symptoms peculiar to the sufferer and the unique disturbance of the solids and fluids that produced them. The first of a physician's skills lay in reasoning out what this particular disturbance was, from his knowledge of the sufferer's life and the recent history of the sickness. This was not diagnosis in the modern sense; there was no identification of a single disease process. There was no one-to-one relationship between external events, pathology, symptoms and cure. For although an individual's condition might be given a name, such as pneumonia, because of the resemblance the symptoms bore to those of other sufferers, more important was that it was a condition peculiar to him. It was a deviation from his natural state. Nor were conditions, even when given a name, constant in their identity. Through improper management a disorder might pass into some other condition. Arthritis could turn inwards and give rise to a stomach complaint, the 'matter' causing pneumonia might leave the lungs and flow or translate to produce liver disease (Nicolson 1988). Consequently the physician's prime therapeutic skill was management: the ability to maintain the balance of his patron's body; to regulate the fluids, to restore harmony and keep what was inside the skin in concord with the outside world. To do this a detailed acquaintance with the sufferer's lifestyle was essential, as was theoretical knowledge of nature's healing powers. To this had to be added knowledge of the action of drugs and the results of physical remedies, such as bleeding.

In therapy, the distinction between the physician's book-learning and the manual skills of other medical attendants became clear. If drugs or surgery were required, and drugs usually were, the physician would either *write* a prescription to be taken to an apothecary who would *prepare* it, or he would call in a surgeon who would *cut* (most commonly perform a blood-letting). Thoughtfully prescribed therapy could deplete the body which was in excess or restore it (notably by diet) when it was in deficit. Either way the aim was to return it to its own natural state.

This was a medicine for wealthy individuals. Sufferers needed time and money for such attentions and they expected their medical attendants, when not their equals in breeding or station, at least to possess the general accomplishments and special learning which could only be acquired by a university education (preferably at Oxford or Cambridge).[3] It was the medical needs of the wealthy, in the end, which dictated the form and substance of orthodox medical knowledge and practice (Jewson 1974; Porter, R. and Porter, D. 1988; Porter, D. and Porter, R. 1989). This is not to say that the meanings of sickness were confined to this, by no means simple, secular framework. Interpretations of illness could be crammed with religious meanings. In the eighteenth century the orthodox held that, in God's creation, the natural and the moral law were one. As the widely read cleric William Paley was to argue towards the end of the century, the poor had a natural place in society and it was their moral duty to stay there. Out of their proper place the poor were rogues and vagrants. Naturally too the body was healthy when things were in their proper place. Transgression of the natural laws which produced health, by overeating, drunkenness or promiscuity, for example, led to a similar moral chaos, signalled by vomiting, sweating or diarrhoea; by matter out of place (Douglas 1966). Sickness could thus be a sign of sin. Orthodox accounts of the body and disease, like eighteenth-century accounts of society itself, were steeped in the language of place and order.

Surgeons, like physicians, were full-time healers, and, again like physicians, were concerned to regulate the practice they claimed to superintend. Whereas physicians attempted to run a kingdom from their College in London, surgeons had no such monarchical organization. They combined in local corporations overseeing practice in the vicinity. The grandest of these corporations were in London and Edinburgh. Surgeons looked different from different perspectives. From the physicians' viewpoint they were an inferior crew. Trained by apprenticeship, like coopers or carpenters, they appeared relatively illiterate folk who worked with their hands. Many members of the

London Company were indeed comparatively unlettered. Until 1745 the Surgeons' Company was united with that of the barbers and many men made a living practising barbering and minor surgery such as blood-letting. Even when they disdained barbering, most surgeons were relatively limited in their manual skills and rarely went beyond such things as lancing abscesses, dressing ulcers and bandaging (Loudon 1986).

Surgical knowledge was deemed by physicians to be confined to those matters obvious to the senses, equipping surgeons to deal only with the tangible and visible, with external diseases, lumps and bumps and broken bones. Such knowledge, said physicians, could be gained by experience alone. Surgeons had not, and did not need, that learning and accomplishment in reasoning which allowed the physician to arrive at hidden causes. They treated not individual disturbances, but specific diseases; after all, one wart was very much like another. At least this is what the physicians said, and it was on this basis that physicians, proclaiming themselves the head of all medicine, attempted to regulate surgical practice. Some surgeons saw things rather differently. The larger cities of the kingdom, London and Edinburgh in particular, contained élites of highly skilled surgeons who despised the ruder aspects of their trade and valued a tradition which they traced to antiquity. They prided themselves on their book-learning and on their detailed anatomical knowledge gained by dissection. This knowledge, they declared, was integral to their practice. Such men could remove stones from bladders, cut off cancerous breasts, amputate gangrenous limbs, set severe fractures and mend broken skulls by trepanning, all with a fair degree of success. It should be observed, however, that even these disorders were considered external, that is, obvious to the surgeon's senses. A stone in the bladder could still be touched through the urethra by what was called a sound, a thin metal probe. Diseases of the true interior of the body, meaning those treated by physicians, were by definition not accessible to the senses, and thus could not be surgical.[4] Cases of syphilis, which all agreed had external manifestations and internal changes, were bitterly contested between physicians and surgeons.

The only other group of healers to be combined in a recognized corporation were the apothecaries. Once upon a time these tradesmen had been dispensers of drugs for physicians. Although they continued in this role, by the eighteenth century many were practising internal medicine and prescribing of their own accord: much to the annoyance of the physicians. They generally treated a humbler clientele than that attended to by physicians and they charged less. Although they were apprentice-trained, like the physicians they practised physic, drawing on the literature of orthodox medicine. The apothecary's progress into the role of general medical practitioner treating those of modest means was part of a change in the social relations of medical men in the eighteenth century. The élite corporations of physicians, surgeons and apothecaries were increasingly unable to police the practices they superintended. Everywhere surgeons, apothecaries and men with some orthodox medical training but no degree or licence, indiscriminately practised physic and surgery. A new medical man, at first called the surgeon-apothecary and then general practitioner, was making a space for himself. This was not a phenomenon peculiar to medicine. The economic buoyancy, relative peace and population growth of the eighteenth century made it possible for a number of modest, self-consciously 'professional' groups to flourish: teachers, lawyers, estate managers and authors for example (Holmes 1982). In the case of medicine it is possible to describe reasonably precisely the factors which allowed this social regrouping to occur. The economic conditions of the eighteenth century, combined with the possibility of social mobility, fostered commercialization and consumerism (McKendrick 1982). Everywhere potters, painters, barbers, manufacturers and tradesmen became entrepreneurs and began to market their commodities or themselves. Mass production (of a sort), advertising and innovation became the rule. Medical goods and medical practice were no exception to this social and cultural transformation. Indeed medicine possessed distinct advantages as a marketable commodity. The idea of perfectibility which characterized so much Enlightenment writing was particularly obvious when authors dwelt on the possibility of improving the physical quality of human life (Passmore 1970). A reconsideration of Christian values was central to this optimism. Since its advent, Christianity in the West had frequently been associated with the devaluation of bodily pleasures: indeed Christians had often encouraged mortification of the flesh. Seventeenth-century Puritans frowned on indulgence in things of the body. But many Enlightenment authors, whether religious or not, stood this thinking on its head. God (or perhaps nature), they said, had fabricated the human body in order that man might enjoy, albeit temperately, the pleasures of creation. Even though many writers deplored what they saw as the spread of gross luxury, the pursuit of modest material comfort and corporeal satisfaction was no longer widely condemned as a sinful activity. Perfectibilist writers, religious or otherwise, turned to the new science of the seventeenth century (natural philosophy as it was called) and paraded it as the instrument of progress. Through the study of the natural laws of the body, society and the universe, they said, would come progress and well-being. Medicine, as might be guessed, came out of all this rather well. During the Enlightenment medical knowledge was employed to explain the virtuous possibilities of material pleasure. Doctors and others developed a language which characterised social progress in terms of the increasing sensibility of the mind and nerves (Barker-Benfield 1992). Sensibility was described as both a physical property of the nervous system and a capacity of the mind to feel. The heightened sensibility found among civilized peoples could be measured by their modest enjoyment of luxury goods. This is one instance of the ways in which, since around 1700, medical categories have increasingly been used as an explanatory resource in western culture. In this case they were being employed to explain and endorse the commerce and consumerism of eighteenth-century life.

In this context the pursuit of health was increasingly viewed by many writers as a good, as an end in itself. The last few decades of the century overflowed with manuals, many written by medical men, replete with details of how the individual was to organize such things as diet, exercise, even the site of his home, so as to ensure health and, implicitly, prosperity.[5] Indeed, by 1800, doctors and others were complaining that they were living in a hypochondriacal society, so visible had medicine become as a unit of cultural currency (Porter, R. 1991). It was this possible market for health that the new order of healers, the general practitioners, began to exploit.

They were not alone. A multitude of other healers, many with no orthodox training whatsoever, some of them itinerants, swarmed through eighteenth-century society. Such men were branded 'quacks' and denounced by both élite and rank-and-file medical men. These 'quacks', however, were usually one step ahead, adopting and adapting the latest theories and appliances of orthodox medicine itself – the electrical machine, mud baths, hot springs, the mesmeric tub, the celestial bed – to bring their healing powers to public attention (Porter, R. 1989a). They employed the technologies of commercialization, notably the press, to advertise the power of their remedies. In the treatment of syphilis they excelled: sufferers from the so-called secret but widespread disease were targeted by those marketing secret remedies. The doctors were driven to despair by these men who were seemingly taking the bread from their mouths. Yet the doctors themselves were far from renouncing the tricks of the healing trade, as the eponymous James's powder and Radcliffe's Royal Tincture testify (James and Radcliffe were distinguished physicians). Besides, if these so-called quacks could produce results and cures that, in the consumer's eyes, compared favourably with those of regular medicine, who was to say who should and who should not practise medicine? On what basis did medical men claim to be authorities in matters of healing, and why should anyone believe them?

One thing that regular practitioners had on their side was just that: being regular. Having a degree or a licence counted for something in many spheres of eighteenth-century life. Eighteenth-century society did formally recognize a medical orthodoxy. The physicians did have privileges protected by Royal Charter. Orthodox medical and surgical texts were valued as part of the literature of élite and middling culture. The universities, Oxford and Cambridge, were the educational institutions through which the ruling class reproduced its cultural forms, training men to fill positions in the church, the law and medicine. Although the place of the doctor in eighteenth-century life was marginal compared to that of the parson, the justice of the peace or the military officer, orthodox medicine was still integral to, if not a particularly potent part of, establishment culture and society. But in a ferociously competitive market, being orthodox was not enough to ensure successful practice. Surgeon-apothecaries, who had to compete with each other and with irregulars, adopted a strategy from the physicians. They began to claim that they had virtues as practitioners not only because they had experience of a *trade*, but because they had learned from books or from great teachers who themselves were book-learned. The London surgeons' break with the barbers and the formation of a separate Company of Surgeons in 1745 was a sign of this change. These practitioners were claiming that their understanding of the *principles* of the healing art ought to give them preference in the market place. The surgeon-apothecaries ran a war on two fronts: on the one they fought competition from the quacks and on the other they assaulted the élite physician's domain. Soon their claims for preference would become a plea for legal privilege.

The first institution to seize the initiative and cater to this new demand for medical learning was the University of Edinburgh. Scotland, economically depressed after the Union with England of 1707, was divided into factions over the best course for the country's future. In Edinburgh, however, a small number of Anglophile Scots, well-connected to London by way of the great Whig clan, the Argylls, seized upon the Union as an opportunity to revive the capital economically by reinvigorating the town's college and creating a medical school. Part of the plan was to keep at home all those Scots who spent money abroad, crossing the North Sea to study in Holland. The school was founded in 1726. Unlike Oxbridge, Edinburgh had no religious test and admitted any man who could pay the matriculation and individual course fees. The university required adherence to no particular curriculum. Students could choose to attend just one course if they wished; many did. Almost from the beginning Edinburgh served more than a local clientele. Students flocked to the city from south of the border, Ireland and, eventually, from America. Many were Dissenters, such as Unitarians and Quakers, the descendants of seventeenth-century religious sectaries. Denied an education at the English universities, as well as careers in parliament, the law, and, obviously, the church, Dissenters turned to commerce and medicine (Raistrick 1968). These enterprises shared features which Dissenters prized. Both could be engaged in as intensely practical activities and both could be considered socially useful. Indeed, success in either of them was considered by Dissenters a sign of worth. Yet another aspect of these activities fitted the dissenting ethos. Both commerce and medicine were held to be progressive, or improvable through the pursuit and application of natural knowledge, or science. Denied positions in the church and the law, Dissenters neglected the cultural ornament – the fine arts – cultivated by those who filled these positions. Dissenters turned instead to the cultivation of the natural sciences as the means to personal and social improvement and, crucial for them, to political reform (Thackray 1974). What better pursuit then for a young Dissenter than commerce or the study and practice of medicine?

At first the Edinburgh courses were modelled rather stiffly on those of the successful Dutch medical school at Leiden. Two professors taught very traditional theory of physic in Latin, and attracted few students. The big draw in these early years was the anatomy classes. These were taught in English by the surgeon and professor, Alexander Monro. Using a couple of corpses each year and dozens of wax models, Monro taught students that a knowledge of anatomy and an understanding of the workings of the body were the basis of sound medical and surgical practice (Lawrence, C. 1988a). Students seemingly held this to be the case too. Monro's classes were filled with surgeons and apothecaries who had finished their apprenticeship and were seeking further improvement and also with men who were putting together a piecemeal medical education. Many of these students came to Edinburgh for a year only and left to practise in the army, the royal and merchant navies or in the expanding towns of England and America (Rosner 1991). The men who came to Edinburgh valued medical learning and so, seemingly, did those whom they eventually attended as practitioners (Lawrence, C. 1985a).

The Edinburgh University medical school had a local as well as a national audience, for its teachers were also key agents in that vigorous cultural self-examination (and Anglicization) known as the Scottish Enlightenment. The professors at the school in the mid-eighteenth century, William Cullen, Joseph Black, Alexander Monro and his son of the same name, hobnobbed with the great literati such as David Hume and Adam Smith. Their message, that through the application of natural knowledge would come improvement, was music to the ears of lowland landlords as well as to dissenting medical students of modest means (Lawrence, C. 1979). The Edinburgh teachers who shaped this message had a sharp eye for demand. They began to lecture in English rather than in Latin, extended the range and number of courses, kept them up to date and, as we shall see, began to shift the emphasis in the understanding of disease in ways which would suit the experiences of the aspiring practitioners they taught.

To change ideas about disease, however, was not to remain Edinburgh's prerogative. The London corporations, notably the College of Physicians and the Company of Surgeons, retained a lazy grip on local medical practice in the first half of the century. The Surgeons' Company licensed apprentices who had served their time and wished to practise in London or in the Navy. It had a remit to teach anatomy, but scarcely exploited it. With no university, London had no other formal institution through which anatomy or medicine might be taught to the new consumers of medical ideas who were beginning to trek North. There was a space, therefore, for enterprising private teachers. London offered the perfect opportunity for such men. The city was a potential magnet for students and, unlike Edinburgh's cramped 'old town', local geography lent itself to expansion: by mid-century the 'west end' was being populated by the fashionable. Private teachers and popular lecturers of all sorts flourished in London. Dancing masters, music and art teachers, and demonstrators of natural philosophy rubbed shoulders with raree-shows, museums, theatres and cock-pits. An audience was guaranteed to the medical man who could market himself and his product. One of the first men to do this, and do it more successfully than any other medical figure of the century, was a Scot, William Hunter. Hunter was a lowlander, initially a surgeon who, after a short stay in Edinburgh, quickly realized that the university teachers there had monopolized the market. Hunter headed for London to make his fortune, which he duly did. Before embarking on his London career, Hunter studied briefly in Paris where, in the massive and overcrowded hospitals, most students learning anatomy had the opportunity to dissect a corpse. Hunter used this experience as a marketing strategy when he opened a private anatomy school in London in 1746. Hunter advertised his anatomical and his surgical teaching and also the opportunity for students to learn in the 'Paris Manner'; that is, to dissect a corpse for themselves (Gelfand 1972). Hunter increasingly coined in the guineas as surgeons and apprentices filled his theatre. Before long he had numerous competitors but Hunter always remained ahead of his rivals. As other anatomists began to open schools Hunter advertised his contacts, his skills in dissection and his anatomical discoveries in order to keep preeminent the school which was becoming such a valuable property. If we look at medicine for a moment, not as a healing art but as a commodity, Hunter appears like any one of a thousand ambitious entrepreneurs making and marketing themselves in the bustle of London. He was careful, it might be added, as were so many successful entrepreneurs, to find someone to give him a leg up. The whole of his career reveals attachments to a number of influential patrons (Porter, R. 1985a).

By the 1770s, London was competing vigorously with Edinburgh as a centre of medical education. It was a vast emporium for medical goods of all kinds; a market place for orthodox and unorthodox healers, a city bursting with private medical schools teaching not just anatomy, but botany, chemistry and medicine itself. This was not all: an entirely new subject, midwifery, appeared as an object of tuition. Medical works since antiquity had discussed diseases of women, and anatomical texts had described and debated the development of the foetus. But the delivery of children, as we have noted, was a female preserve, indeed many midwives were licensed by episcopal authorities. Gradually during the eighteenth century, more and more women who could afford the expense employed a so-called man-midwife, or *accoucheur*. These men were surgeons and physicians who not only attended desperate cases but were increasingly present at uncomplicated deliveries. Once again, William Hunter was one of those who saw a market; this time for the *accoucheur*. Hunter was not the first man-midwife, but he was to become one of the most famous expositors of the art. Hunter gave classes in midwifery for surgeons and midwives and attended and assisted at the confinements of the wealthy. By the end of the century the new breed of surgeon-apothecaries (who, unlike women, were allowed to use the recently invented forceps), were endeavouring to edge out traditional midwifery and replace it with what they deemed rational, principled practice. How had this come about? Both economic and cultural factors were at work. First the market; throughout the century medical men were active exploiters of any potential space into which they might expand their practice and in the instance of midwifery they simply turned to further use the entrée they already had by virtue of their attendance at tricky cases. But why was this expansion permitted? Culturally, midwifery was ripe for medical reinterpretation. As we have noted, medical texts had long discoursed on pregnancy. But Enlightenment sentiments made it easy for medical men to represent traditional practices as steeped in superstition, needing reform and the guidance of principled art. Only through rational understanding, through knowledge of anatomy and physiology, men like William Hunter declared, could midwifery become safe. The new midwifery was, indeed, different in practice. Curtains were opened, light and air admitted, the husband was permitted to enter; a theatre was created where, so the man-midwife said, *nature*, not prejudice, could take its course. Among the élite of London society such sentiments and practices seemed progressive; they had a sympathetic hearing and soon found favour with literate men and women of middling means (Donnison 1977; Wilson 1985b).

This Enlightenment sensibility, which esteemed what it saw as rational improvement, coincided with medical interests in another area: the founding of hospitals. During the eighteenth century, the foundation and reform of institutions – gaols, schools, workhouses, foundling hospitals – was promoted as a much valued goal by improving, this-worldly thinkers. Within such places they said, the poor could be supervised, reformed, shown their place in the social order, taught gratitude to their betters and the value of labour; by such means, moral progress and gradual improvement of the whole would be brought about (Ignatieff 1978). Medicine could be exploited for, and lent itself to, the pursuit of such ends. Unlike religion or politics, the source of much previous and ongoing strife, medicine, as we have seen, was deemed by Enlightenment thinkers to have the potential to deliver this-worldly happiness. It was a cultural formation around which people of different persuasions might coalesce in the promotion of what they accounted the local and the general good. And this, to some extent, is what happened. After the founding of the Westminster Hospital in London in 1719, similar institutions soon sprang up in the metropolis. When the Winchester County Hospital was founded in 1736, the provinces followed suit. Five major hospitals were established in London before 1745, and any modest-sized town which, at the end of the century, did not have its own hospital could count itself backward. Patterns of foundation varied of course. The Westminster was the product of local Tory support, Guy's was the result of a posthumous bequest, in others Church of England or the dissenting interest prevailed. But in many places the local infirmary, or voluntary hospital as it was called, was the product of co-operative philanthropy, in which subscribers came from nearly all parts of that political and religious spectrum which spanned the middle and upper orders (Owen 1965; Woodward 1974).

Hospitals were not founded as a response to industrialization and a diseased proletariat: far from it (Webster 1978). Most were small-scale solutions to local concerns about the related issues of sickness, poverty and disorder, although founders and subscribers also perceived organized charity to be a new instrument for the promotion of national ends (Andrew 1989). Hospitals flourished in towns and cities where landed wealth and newer commercial interests combined to make patronage and paternalism the order of the day. Hospitals, indeed, were demonstrations of that ordering and sites for the day-to-day reaffirmation of it. Through their infirmaries, the moderately well-off along with the very wealthy could exercise Christian charity and fulfil their duties to the local poor. The poor, in turn, could learn gratitude and deference. Hospitals were not gateways to death, places dreaded by the poor, indeed admission was often much sought after and not easily attained. Infirmaries were, in general, small institutions with few beds. In most instances only the worthy poor, suitably recommended by a subscriber, would be admitted. The hospital institutionalized the face-to-face world of reciprocal obligation that was taken to be, by the rich at least, the proper way of ordering things. The hospital, in the perception of its subscribers, made more rational, more modern, the natural order of society.

There was, however, something new in this, something that was to be a source of great change. The hospital was the setting for the first contact on any scale between the doctors and the poor. In the seventeenth century, London physicians had run a dispensary for the needy. Throughout the early modern period parishes occasionally employed a local surgeon. But the hospital was the site in which medicine was to have its first prominent and ongoing role in the ordering of the lives of the poor. The expansion of that role we will explore in later chapters. Here we should note that, for much of the eighteenth century, medical power within the voluntary hospitals, in the sense of the capacity to influence policy, was relatively limited. Local physicians, surgeons and apothecaries offered their services gratis and part time to such institutions. Positions were much sought after: appointments, made by governors, brought social prominence, contact with subscribers and thus the possibility of lucrative practice. But medical perceptions did not structure the broadest features of hospital life. Most of these institutions were designated by their governors as sites for the treatment of specified, acute (sudden, short-term) diseases only. Rules varied, but, for instance, most hospitals did not admit the chronically (long-term) sick, the aged, the mad or children. This was not a medically-inspired directive. The return of the poor, cured, into the community, figured large in a hospital's humanitarian and economic justification of itself, and acute, but not chronic, disorders might be fairly quickly remedied. These various local concerns with the health of the poor coincided with a national sentiment: that the wealth and strength of the state was to be promoted by increasing the size and health of the population. In the voluntary hospital and such institutions as the Foundling Hospital (dedicated to rescuing unwanted infants), Enlightenment sentiments and economic thinking neatly combined (Andrew 1989).

For the most part eighteenth-century hospitals were well-regarded, certainly by the subscribers. When they did not cure the sick (and most hospitals boasted a good record in this respect) they claimed to do them no harm. Although there is evidence that the poor occasionally voiced fears about being experimented on, or being dissected after death, these were, in the main, horrors of the nineteenth century. Hospital governors had so much control over medical men, so great an interest in representing their institutions as models of benevolence and so great a concern with the spiritual well-being of their charges that the mid-eighteenth-century hospital was in little danger of becoming an exclusively *medical* establishment.

By the end of the century, however, in hospitals, and in many other institutions where the poor were confined or lived or worked, medical men were pressing their claims and beginning to gain a measure of authority and control. To do this medical men developed new models of disease, new modes of practice and new educational forms. In many respects these innovations were borrowings from surgical traditions. The social changes at work generating this development lay in the changing occupational opportunities of doctors. In the second half of the century our new medical men, not quite pure physician not quite pure surgeon, were beginning to find relatively regular employment in areas of expanding manpower, notably the army, the East India Company, and above all, the Royal Navy. It was in these and similar contexts, such as gaols and newly appearing towns, that doctors began to encounter diseases of populations. These diseases were, overwhelmingly the epidemic and endemic fevers (Bynum 1981). As we have seen, ideas about disease employed by orthodox practitioners early in the century can roughly be divided into two sorts. First there was the notion of sickness as a deviation from the sufferer's natural state (the concept used by élite physicians). Although the medical literature did contain plenty of descriptions of epidemic fevers and how they could devastate populations, medical practice was usually orientated to the management of the individual features of a case, whether or not the disease was distinguished as an epidemic fever. Second was the idea of disease as a specific, visible, localized thing, occurring on the surface of the body, and always amenable to the same sort of therapy (the hand of the surgeon). Although an idealization, this model does serve to categorize the approaches doctors had to disease in the eighteenth century. These different concepts, even if not always immediately apparent in practice, also embodied that hierarchical and divided account of medicine given by physicians and, to some extent, surgeons themselves.

Occupationally and conceptually some medical men began to challenge that hierarchy. Subtly but surely, they began to produce new accounts of disease. To begin with the emphasis on the character of disorders began to shift. For example, in Edinburgh, the professor of medicine, William Cullen (once a ship's surgeon), insisted that all diseases could be classified into distinct species, like plants, like surgical disorders indeed. This could be done, he said, if attention was paid to the shared and most obvious characteristics of cases. To arrive at such a classification, Cullen taught, the doctor should acquaint himself with many cases and describe their symptoms. In other words, what was beginning to matter was what two or more sufferers *had in common*, not what made them different. By delineating disease in this way, medical men said, they would be able consistently to identify disorders such as scurvy in a ship's crew, or the low and nervous fever among prisoners. Such a delineation, they added, was the necessary prelude to discovering the causal factors producing the disease. Thus classification was a prerequisite for identifying disease and instituting preventative or curative measures *for an institutional population as a whole*.

In their assertion that they understood the nature and causes of epidemic and endemic disease, medical men were claiming an ability to restore and maintain order among a populace. It was this claimed ability that they used to promote their advancement. Their ability to restore order, medical men said, rested on their understanding of the causes of the diseases they had delineated. In fact, to describe the origins of sickness in populations, medical men used a version of the model which they applied to the individual sufferer. Multiple factors: diet, climate, living conditions and so forth, they said, conspired in particular situations to bring about an outbreak of this or that fever in a population (Hamlin 1992). In some situations, notably in towns, some observers saw poverty to be the root cause of outbreaks of fever. Late eighteenth-century medical men observed, investigated and reported on epidemics, carefully cataloguing their clinical course and circumstantial features. The medical literature abounds with accounts by, say, naval surgeons, of outbreaks of fever in ships' crews. Symptoms were reported in detail and great attention was paid to such things as prevailing meteorological conditions, diet and morale. Relatively new to this enquiry, however, was a stress on the causal role of dirt, moral laxity and indolence. Prior to the eighteenth century, dirt, although it was sometimes identified with disease causation, primarily had aesthetic and religious connotations. Eighteenth-century doctors, however, began to emphasize the role of dirt as a significant pathological agent. Dirt, they were saying, signified disorder, whereas cleanliness signified order and, necessarily, morality.[6] 'Cleanliness', the physician, Sir John Pringle, explained, 'is conducive to health but is it not obvious that it also tends to good order and other virtues?' (Temkin 1977). In the development of this new clinical and causal model of epidemic disease we can see how traditional medicine was being shaped by a new group of doctors to explain and effect the ordering of large institutions (Hannaway 1981). This change is nowhere better illustrated than in the activities of medical men in the eighteenth-century Royal Navy.

For most of the eighteenth-century the ship's surgeon was a relatively humble figure, not even a commissioned officer, as Smollett's *Roderick Random* testifies. His job was almost entirely curative, mainly treating venereal disease or amputating limbs during battle. James Cook's much reported voyages of the late 1760s and 1770s represent a significant moment of transition to a new account of medicine afloat. Cook's small ships were run immensely successfully and Cook himself was seen as a model paternalist. Yet although Cook's success was seen in terms of his 'fatherly' care of his crew, it was also attributed by him, and others, to his ability to maintain order by enforcing cleanliness. The language of order and cleanliness used by Cook, however, was one which was being elaborated by medical men, such as Sir John Pringle, President of the Royal Society. Pringle, formerly Physician General to the army, was the author of works on the diseases of prisons and military camps. Through his position in the Society, Pringle injected the new medicine into Cook's explorations.

For reasons of distance, amongst others, the Navy was relatively ineffectual during the American Revolutionary war. But at the turn of the century, during the wars with France, the Royal Navy, one of the 'sinews of power' of the state, was the foundation of British success (Brewer 1988). By this time the Navy was a massive enterprise. Ships were manned by as many as a thousand souls whose vitality depended on a huge industrial infrastructure of dockyards, victualling machinery and so forth. In this context medical men increasingly pressed their claims to be important agents of discipline. Disorder, or the threat of it, and disease, they said, were shipmates. For example, in 1806, a naval surgeon noted that, 'attention to discipline should be more particularly observed in ships that contain a number of impressed men. . . Among this class of people scurvy is most apt to break out' (Lawrence, C. 1994). The most vocal spokesmen for the new medicine described the surgeon's role as writing reports, compiling statistics, inspecting between decks, rather than simply practising curative medicine. Preventative medicine, they argued, should be a cornerstone of naval discipline. Medical supervision to produce order and cleanliness, combined with sound diet, would result in efficiency and moral improvement. Naval medical men were turning the success of Cook's voyages to good use. They were working out a supervisory role for medicine, just as new disciplinary models were being elaborated in prisons and factories. Naval surgeons were, indeed, given an increasingly large supervisory role and their reward came in 1806 with their elevation to the quarterdeck, that part of the ship reserved for commissioned officers.

On land there were related developments. In London and elsewhere physicians and surgeons, with the consent of the governors, began to use hospitals as institutional bases for creating private schools of medicine. Here they taught the same subjects that other private teachers taught in their lecture rooms. But in addition many physicians and surgeons with hospital appointments, again with the consent of the governors, began to use their institutions as sites for clinical instruction. In Edinburgh, when clinical teaching began in 1748, the professor, John Rutherford, taught very traditional physic. The bodies of the poor were being used to teach students the sort of medicine they would practise on the wealthy. Such clinical teaching was a luxury and classes were attended by only a few students. By the beginning of the next century this innovation had been built on and transformed. Students filled the wards of many of the large hospitals. The teachers imparted new classifications of disease, such as Cullen's, and stressed the importance of clinical experience in the learning and advancement of medicine and surgery. This was new. Physicians had, of course, always applauded bedside observation, and, in this respect had never ceased to evoke the name of Hippocrates. But the insistence on the importance of clinical instruction in a setting where many patients were gathered together – the hospital – was virtually unprecedented (Park 1991).

2　The age of reform

Although orthodox medicine's hierarchical structure　might have seemed, to some, to be changing in the late eighteenth century, élite medicine remained a significant feature of the social and cultural landscape. During the years of the French wars the medical and surgical élites used their connections, their institutions and their account of the natural ordering of things, especially of the body and disease, in the interests of conservatism and reaction. In many ways they held fast to the medical and social orderings of the eighteenth century. The great medical corporations remained their seats of power. In London, the College of Physicians still recruited its Fellows from Oxbridge and the members of the council of the Company of Surgeons (Royal College after 1800) were among the wealthiest of metropolitan practitioners. In Edinburgh, the medical school and the College of Physicians were binary stars which ensured that appointments to vacant chairs went to suitable Tory candidates, especially if they belonged to one of the local medical families. In some ways élite medical men consolidated their power in these years. In London and Edinburgh they made headway in controlling the expanding great hospitals where they held visiting appointments and monopolized the teaching. Their conservatism is hardly surprising. They conversed with hospital governors and hob-nobbed with the affluent and the aristocracy. Just as in the Enlighten-ment, their clientele chose them for their manners and their gentlemanly conduct as much as for their medical know-how. Not surprisingly such physicians and surgeons were, in the main, Tory and Church of England or Scotland.

Eighteenth-century economic opportunity and Enlightenment rational-ism and optimism, however, had spawned far too many medical competitors for the élite to ignore them. During the war years these new medical men began to organize themselves in societies, articulate their grievances more loudly and challenge the hegemony of the old order more forcefully. These new doctors, the general practitioners, were surgeons, apothecaries (or both) and Scottish trained MDs. For the most part they had put together their occupational skills by combining apprenticeship and self-education: taking classes in medicine, anatomy, chemistry and midwifery in the private London schools, walking the wards of the London hospitals and attending the University of Edinburgh (Loudon 1986). But this latter institution had, it seemed to many, ossified, and in private schools in the northern capital and in that city's College of Surgeons (the least conservative of all the corporations) other teachers seized the initiative and were teaching anatomical and medical ideas which they had imported from France (Lawrence 1988b; Jacyna 1994).

For the most part this new strain of medical men did not fare too badly during the wars. After all, the Navy and the military were sources of employment. None the less, they did feel themselves squeezed. From above, the medical élite endeavoured to control their practice. From below (at least as they saw it), quacks, commercial medicine manufacturers and, increasingly, druggists (later dispensing chemists) were competing for trade. General practitioners were, in many useful senses of the phrase, in the middle. Their patients were the middling orders (the poor could not pay) and many of them promoted and cultivated reformist causes inimical to the culture of élite medicine. To further their interests they pressed the case for having a say in the running of medicine and, more radically, for a closed (bounded), single profession. They pursued anatomy, chemistry and physiology and insisted that this learning fitted them alone to be recognized as practitioners of medicine (French and Wear 1991). Here we see the appearance of a claim to privilege for an occupationally closed, meritocratically organized body of experts; a claim that was often voiced in Victorian society. In their stress on the importance of clinical training in hospitals and their emphasis on the value of statistics we see the shaping of a medicine for curing and ordering the poor. In their denunciation of learned physic in the name of observational science we see an attack on the medicine they associated with élites and the announcement of what some saw as a new medicine for a new social order. These men were not, for the most part, political radicals. They were not especially associated with corresponding societies or fervent advocates of French Revolutionary ideals. Quite often the reverse was the case. Even when they were radical in some areas, as was the democrat Thomas Beddoes, they were not outright opponents of all privilege. Beddoes, a Bristol practitioner and friend of Samuel Taylor Coleridge in his young, radical days of the 1790s, campaigned for democratic reform of parliament (Stansfield

1984; Porter, R. 1992). But Beddoes's writings also employed the language of a new subject: medical police. Developed by doctors in the German states and in France, medical police (from the Greek, *politeia*, the constitution of a state) prescribed a key role for medical men as students and managers of society (Rosen 1974; Jordanova 1981). A rationally organized society, so the texts on medical police said, would be based on knowledge of how men's minds, and thus their morals, were produced from the social and physical environment in which they lived. Who better to study this and prescribe for change, the texts went on, than a single body of professional medical men?

Central to many of the reshapings of medicine which were occurring at this time were refashionings of medical knowledge. Medical men differed over the control and organization of this, just as they did over medical practice. The era of the Napoleonic Wars and the thirty years following were characterized by intense conflict over the constitution of such things as anatomical, physiological and pathological facts and, more broadly, the method appropriate to the production of those facts and the theories the facts were used to sustain. These were not only academic disputes: quite the reverse. Arguments about the constitution of medical knowledge were arguments, very often public, about the organization of society. Medical men and others built into their models of the body and disease prescriptions for maintaining or changing the social order. As we have seen, elite concepts of the body and disease in the eighteenth century dwelt on the importance of harmony, of natural place and the serious consequences of bodily matter crossing its proper boundaries. These concerns spoke to the patronage-based, hierarchical society of the Enlightenment. Similar concerns remained in nineteenth-century medical thought, but equally important were claims for fundamentally reorganizing bodily knowledge, for breaking with the past and for constituting knowledge, and thus society, anew.

One of the best known reorderings of knowledge produced at this time was organology or cranioscopy, later called phrenology. This comprised an account of the brain and an associated method of investigating it. Conceptually, phrenology was the child of an Austrian anatomist, Franz Joseph Gall, who began his work in the 1790s. Its continental history is relatively unimportant here, except to note that in France, during the Empire and Restoration, it was perceived as a highly dangerous, radical, political philosophy (Jacyna 1987). It had much of that taint in Britain. Phrenology was based on a fundamentally new model of the nervous system and its most contested conclusion was that different parts of the brain were essential for the action of the faculties of the mind. This action phrenologists said, could be practically investigated by inspecting or feeling the size of the cranial contours, the bumps on the skull (cranioscopy). Such size they declared, revealed the degree of development of the various mental faculties. Phrenology in Britain was launched on its career well before the end of the Napoleonic Wars. To the establishment, whose view could be heard in the voices of the medical élite, phrenology was an utterly fallacious body of knowledge. The view that the brain might be sufficient to produce the actions of mind seemed a threat to the doctrine of the immortality of soul and, in turn, to organized religion and the social order.[1] To many of its protagonists, however, phrenology demonstrated that the basis of human activity lay solely in natural laws and it prescribed how, by gaining knowledge of those laws, human beings could bring about rational, progressive change. To them it was the first true science of mind, a science grounded in the anatomy of the nervous system (Shapin 1979).

Who were these phrenologists? For the most part they were drawn from the middling and lower-middling orders; to call them classes is to give them an identity they did not yet quite feel themselves. They were the backbone of provincial culture: wealthier artisans, small tradesmen, lawyers, school teachers and many of our new medical men. Phrenology legitimized, in natural law, the aspirations of these men, excluded, as they saw it, from power in every quarter (Cooter 1984). Of course not all general practitioners endorsed phrenology, still less its most radical versions. Many general practitioners embraced conservative philosophies hostile to phrenology, Tory paternalism or evangelicalism for example (Hilton 1988). Here they were at one with medical élite. Phrenology did not flourish in the University of Edinburgh or at the Colleges of Surgeons or Physicians, far from it, but in the extramural classes of the northern capital and in the private London medical schools (although not those attached to the great hospitals). Later it would thrive in mechanics' institutes and in phrenological societies.

Phrenology, because of the overt political sentiments it generated, is the most florid example of a cognitive revolution that was being effected at this time. Phrenology shared with other sciences that were being created the abandonment of many Enlightenment assumptions about the constitution of knowledge. In some respects natural history, in the sense of recording and classifying the visible, was characteristic of knowledge produced during the Enlightenment (Sloan 1990). Cullen's view of how diseases should be identified and classified, that is by their symptoms, fits this account. This natural historical approach to understanding the world was abandoned (or at least made marginal or subsidiary) in the years following the French revolution in favour of knowledge of deep structure, such as archetypal plan in the case of comparative anatomy or strata in the instance of the new science of geology. The priority given to knowledge as classification of visible surface features, was overturned. Significant knowledge was now deemed knowledge of hidden organization (or in medicine, disorganization as well) (Foucault 1970).[2] In geology, the animal kingdom and human society itself, this idea of depth increasingly came to encompass knowledge of the past, of the historical in a temporal sense. This reordering extended to knowledge of disease. Doctors began to search, by post-mortem examination, deep in the body for disorganized anatomy. This morbid anatomy, which they found in the dead house, they identified as the basis of those species of disease which, in the Enlightenment, they had begun to describe and classify by their symptoms. This morbid-anatomical knowledge was then used to guide clinical practice; the search *at the bedside* for deep *structural* change, for morbid anatomy, in the living patient. The eighteenth-century physician's practice of reasoning to causes of disease which were, necessarily, invisible and intangible was being replaced by the attempt to give the causes of symptoms physical location: by looking, touching and listening; by constructing in the mind's eye a *picture* of a three-dimensional lesion.[3] Reasoning from the symptoms that the client had weakly acting fibres in the chest was being displaced by detecting with the ear that the patient had a cavity in the lungs. The new approach to disease also had a temporal dimension. By performing many post-mortems, clinicians pictured morbid-anatomical change over time. These changes were held to explain the *course* of a patient's sickness. The idea of a disease process distinct from the sufferer was being shaped.

This transformation in medical knowledge occurred most spectacularly in the massively overcrowded hospitals of Paris (Ackerknecht 1967; Foucault 1973). Here patients could be physically examined with impunity. Their bodies could be touched and listened to. Corpses, where the causes of disease were sought, were available in their thousands. Here doctors developed instruments and techniques for physical examination (the stethoscope, invented in 1816, is the best known example) which they used to seek out and picture among the living the causes of disease they had already *observed* among the dead. Not surprisingly surgeons were foremost in this activity, for this was a surgical view of disease (Temkin 1951). Disease as an individual loss of harmony had no place here, a world which designated physical diagnosis, *locating* pathology with the senses, as the preeminent medical skill. Treatment was a secondary consideration. Paris medicine is a striking illustration of the ways in which the reconstitution of knowledge was central to the doctors' reconstitution of their role in society (Waddington 1973; Jewson 1976). This medicine slowly began to be adopted across the channel, even during the Napoleonic Wars. Most of those who took the first interest in it were medical men outside the élite (Maulitz 1987; Warner 1991).

Grand programmes for the rational reform of society were, of course, far from the minds of most ordinary medical men. They felt themselves talented and trapped. They claimed skills and scientific knowledge and wanted due recognition. Most of all they wanted to keep medicine to themselves. Agitation by the majority of medical men during the war years was narrowly focused on the reform of the organization of medicine itself. To promote this end they lobbied parliament and banded together in societies. A twenty-year story of agitation was not without effect. The Apothecaries' Act of 1815 was the result of the general practitioners' political labours. The Act required the Society of Apothecaries to function as a licensing body for all medical men who did not have an MD or a diploma from the College of Surgeons. It required that candidates for licensure had followed an apprenticeship and had attended classes in various subjects. The Act was significant for a number of reasons. First, although parliament acted reluctantly, it was an indication that the state was prepared to interfere in medicine. Second, seen on the broad canvas, the reformers did achieve the largest of their aims (although they scarcely perceived it like that), namely government reform and some protection. It was a sign that rank-and-file medical agitators did have power to move the establishment. Third, the Act effectively recognized the new breed of general practitioner and required him to have a training of a certain sort, albeit in practice the Act simply made obligatory the sort of education general practitioners had been seeking out voluntarily for the previous ten years (Lawrence, S. 1988). In context, however, most important was the Act's conservatism. It gave nothing like a monopoly of practice to rank-and-file practitioners and nobody, except themselves, remotely thought that it should. It endorsed and increased the power of the ancient corporations and excluded many Scottish trained practitioners. The demand of many doctors that there should be a single profession founded on a single qualification requiring joint education in medicine and surgery (as had been created in France during and after the Revolution) was far too much for the medical élite to swallow.[4] Behind the scenes they stamped their power on the Act as effectively as the landed élites preserved their power in the face of industrial and commercial interests (Holloway 1966).

Medical responses to, and involvement in, the industrialization, urban growth, social disorder and political division of the years 1790–1815 were immensely complex. Medical agitation saw doctors produce a variety of new accounts of the proper place of medical knowledge and practice in understanding and regulating the social order. But varying though these accounts were, all were underpinned by the assumption (often explicit) that orthodox practitioners should be recognized as the legitimate healers of the sick and acknowledged as significant custodians of social order. Orthodox practitioners were unanimous (but far from united) in condemning the unorthodox, but orthodoxy itself was deeply divided between élite and rank-and-file. Although the élite largely identified in behaviour and belief with the establishment, general practitioners were split into every shade of political and religious opinion, united in their sense of exclusion but divided as to the best means forward.

In many ways, by 1815, the character of the struggle within which medical men were to shape their place in society over the next forty years had already been established. There was the contest within orthodoxy, between the élite and the rank-and-file; there was the attempt to control unorthodoxy; there was the appeal on all sides to science; and there was the endeavour in some quarters to make medicine one of the fundamental resources for the rational ordering of industrial society. But if the medical struggle after Waterloo was conducted in much the same terms as it had been before, its intensity was far greater. A great number of medical men experienced the economic depression of these years. The market was flooded with newly discharged military and naval surgeons as well as being the site of fierce competition among regulars, alternative practitioners, druggists and commercial products. The poor could not pay and often the parish would not fund the visit of an orthodox practitioner. Rich patients were creamed off by the élite and the rank-and-file fell over one another to attract the attention of the middle classes and artisans. The poor, however, were not wholly outside the sphere of orthodoxy. General practitioners were increasingly being utilized under the old Poor Law. In the expanding hospitals too there was increasing contact between doctors and the poor (Abel-Smith 1964). Hospital appointments remained gateways to medical respectability. In the great London institutions, positions were in the hands of the most august practitioners, such as the surgeon, Sir Astley Cooper, who practised at Guy's (a minor operation on George IV earned him the baronetcy).[5] Such men looked to their friends, connections and family when seeking colleagues. Elsewhere the more ordinary but presentable practitioner might gain an appointment at one of the smaller infirmaries or one of the many new specialist hospitals. These were sometimes founded by particular groups (such as evangelicals) and admitted patients from a targeted fraction of the population, such as sufferers from venereal disease. Specialist hospitals, for example for diseases of the eye or of the rectum, also began to be founded by doctors as a means to promote their advancement (Granshaw 1985). In one way or another the increasing number of indigents who were admitted to these various charitable institutions generated, and was used to justify, the case for medicine having a place in the management both of the worthy and the less worthy poor.

As we have noted, the struggle for recognition carried on by the more humble practitioners intensified during these years. It is a measure of the increasing prestige attached to natural or scientific knowledge (which was increasingly identified as rational knowledge) that in the struggles between general practitioners and the élite, and between orthodoxy and unorthodoxy, science was projected into an ever more prominent position. All sides claimed to be custodians of the authentic knowledge and methods by which medicine should be improved, even though such authentic knowledge and methods might look quite different according to who was claiming to possess them. That is, as a group, medical men were increasingly identifying science as *the* agent for understanding and ordering the world, yet they contested among themselves and with others the constitution of that science. The political nature of these conflicts was often quite manifest and a particularly flagrant example occurred in 1816–17 after a series of lectures by a young London surgeon, William Lawrence. In England, especially in the London, hospital-based, medical schools, the teaching of physiology was subservient to anatomy. Anatomy classes were, amongst other things, demonstrations of the works of God. The body's parts were designed, said the lecturers, and this fact pointed to a Designer. The body's functions, its physiology, were held to follow from that perfect design. From this perspective the body's workings showed evidence of the existence of an immaterial vital principle. This, in turn, also evidenced the existence of the Deity, since, it was held, mere matter could not give rise to the marvels of life. Lawrence, however, drawing on French authors proposed that body function be studied as the outcome of material organization without any reference to a principle of life.[6] Included in the body's functions, he said, was human thought which should be studied as the product of the action of the brain. Thus, although Lawrence claimed he was pleading for nothing more than an autonomous science of physiology, he was, to his opponents, severing the study of nature from its relations with divinity and morality.

Lawrence's programme was denounced by the establishment. A fellow St Bartholomew's Hospital surgeon, John Abernethy, saw in Lawrence's lectures the spectre of materialism and French radicalism. It savoured of doctrines similar to phrenology, which by now was firmly linked in the establishment's eye with the threat of civil disorder. Abernethy spoke for the voices of reaction. He reaffirmed the links between the study of nature and knowledge of the Creator. His polemic distanced the mind from any material contamination and underlined the role of religion. That this polemic was a defence of the established order hardly needs pointing out (Temkin 1963; Goodfield-Toulmin 1969; Figlio 1976; Jacyna 1983).

Controversies of this sort persisted and intensified over the next twenty years. Disputes, whether about the reform of a medical institution or the truth of a scientific doctrine, were, simultaneously, contests over the adequacy or otherwise of the social order. The Royal College of Surgeons was frequently the locus of such controversies in the thirty years 1820–50. Most general practitioners saw the College as the power base of a privileged minority who looked only to itself and which failed to protect the interests of its less-esteemed members. By the 1820s, these less-esteemed members were far more organized and in command of a radical medical press. The most famous representative of this was the *Lancet*, founded by Thomas Wakley in 1823 and edited by him thereafter. Wakley later became a radical Member of Parliament and a prominent agitator for what were perceived as democratic and populist causes such as the coroner's inquest. The *Lancet* tirelessly lampooned and lambasted the élite practitioners of the great London hospitals and the Royal Colleges.

By the late 1820s London had not only a major medical journal, the Lancet, but also a major institution which differed in character from the institutions run by the Tory medical élite. University College London was founded by an alliance of men who comprised Benthamites, radicals and Whigs, many of whom were advocates of what they claimed were democratic, Scottish, educational ideals. The college was inaugurated in 1826 as a secular institution (it was originally called the London University). From the first its founders intended that it should be the seat, not of polite learning, such as Oxford and Cambridge were deemed to impart, but of useful, professional knowledge at the service of the social reformer. Thus medicine and law were high on the list of priorities. The university soon offered medical classes differing significantly from those of the London hospitals. Far more than most of the teachers at the schools attached to the great hospitals, University College lecturers stressed the role of the basic sciences in medicine. In particular they turned to continental models and favoured thoroughgoing naturalism. Many University College teachers spoke with the voice of middle-class rational reform. The college was established by the same reforming interest which saw in mechanics' institutes a means by which the artisan might, through self-education, be made sober, reliable and industrious (Shapin and Barnes 1977). The founders, however, often got more than they bargained for. For example, in the professor of comparative anatomy, Robert Grant, they had a teacher whose political and anatomical radicalism went far beyond respectable middle-class reforming opinions. University College Hospital opened its doors in 1834 and here, too, radical science was embraced by some of the teachers. Likewise this was occasionally taken further than the college establishment approved. The medical professor, John Elliotson, endorsed the healing powers of mesmerism, a doctrine with radical political associations, precipitating a scandal which led to his resignation in 1838.

In the 1830s the united voice of radical political and medical reform was common in the metropolis. The College of Surgeons came under repeated attack, not simply for its professional élitism but for its conservative science. Comparative anatomy in particular became prominent as a politically contested subject. By this time, a number of private anatomy teachers were infusing their lectures with evolutionist doctrines, specifically those of the French naturalist, Jean Baptiste Lamarck. These teachings, which stated that higher forms developed over time from lower ones, were used to contest doctrines which preached that nature and the social order were created and static. These radical doctrines legitimated the view that social progress could and should be brought about by reform. Such teachings were anathema at the College of Surgeons. Here the professor of anatomy, Richard Owen, taught a theory which stated that unchanging Platonic archetypes were the basis of animal morphology. In this way Owen contradicted the possibility of transmutation between species, denying change in nature and thus defending the social *status quo* (Desmond 1989).

In describing the practice of medicine during the decades immediately following the Napoleonic Wars it is important that the historian should not lapse into such expressions as 'medicine was divided' or in a 'state of division'. Such a shorthand description posits some whole, self-contained, bounded object, 'medicine', which is thus credited with having existed historically. The *practice* of medicine, healing and caring for the sick in the post-Napoleonic period, was enormously diverse. The Apothecaries' Act threw some rough and ready girdle around one body of men but it also divided them. In addition many doctors legitimately qualified under the Act practised medicine in ways which seemed outrageous to those who deemed themselves the champions of orthodoxy. Regular medical men could be found employing approaches often associated with subversive practitioners, for example, homeopathy, hydrotherapy and electrical therapy. None of these practices, however, maps regularly on to any obvious political grouping. There were those who developed homeopathic views in line with Whig ideals, and those who gave them radical reformist and religious twists (Rankin 1988). Mesmerism, however, another medical therapy, usually appeared in radical form. In the hands of women such as Harriet Martineau, a political writer, it become a locus of resistance to what was perceived as the increasingly constrained world of middle-class, female life. Martineau's adoption of mesmerism as a cure for her complaints (which orthodox medical men denounced as 'frenzied fantasies') serves to make another point (Cooter 1991). As we have observed several times, the doctor was not the uncontested custodian of medical doctrines and practice. At first glance, therefore, there are many similarities between the 1830s and the late eighteenth century, for in both periods unorthodox healers abounded and commercialism ran riot. In the 1830s healers presented their credentials as herbalists, electricians, phreno-mesmerists, and increasingly, as in the case of the Coffinites (followers of the medical botanist Albert Isaiah Coffin), as importers of American fashions (Cooter 1988). Likewise, in both periods, domestic medical texts and advice manuals flooded the market. Yet there were important differences between the Victorian and the earlier Georgian world. In the Enlightenment, the medical market place was the hunting ground of the individual entrepreneur. The ambitious outsider, with an eye to making money from healing, made a collage of medical doctrines and practices and marketed it as his personal product. The country teemed with healers, flamboyantly selling their medical wares and, if they were successful, they achieved respectability and rode in carriages bearing their arms. Even the most outrageous healers, if they got lucky, could associate with the gentry and aristocracy. They looked, indeed, like the most successful physicians. Anyone clever enough to clamber up the pole of patronage could get rich through medicine.

The tone of nineteenth-century alternative practice was different from this. Deep down among the pauper classes it is impossible to know what constituted the healing arts. Among those who could pay, however, healing rarely came alone. It did not come as it most commonly did in the Enlightenment, from the individual only; the huckster, the showman, the doctor, the itinerant, the patent-medicine seller, the quack. It came from a sect, rationally informed, loaded with moral earnestness and bent on promoting political conservatism or reform, teetotalism, evangelicalism or atheism (an observation which is just as true of orthodox medicine, if it is thought of as simply another sect or, better, group of sects). There were, of course, eighteenth-century precedents for this. John Wesley brought Methodism to the people by way of healing, and many Dissenters, such as John Coakley Lettsom and his circle, carried their own varieties of earnestness and moral reform in their medicine (Marcovich 1982). But in the nineteenth century what had formerly been the exception became the norm. From a distant perspective, what is striking about the medical doctrines created during the industrial revolution is what they have in common. Most applauded the virtues of self-education; all (or nearly all) proclaimed that knowledge of anatomy and physiology was the basis of health; all promised that through understanding, meaning rational or scientific understanding, disease would be conquered; and all posited that such understanding was the consequence of naturalistic enquiry by a medical élite (the medical botanists were an important exception to this last point) (Miley and Pickstone 1988).

If, however, we now view these things from an intermediate position, not so close that we see only the diversity of medical practice, nor so far away that we see only the things all medical practices shared, we can focus, very roughly, on what it was that the regulars had in common. From this position we can see that the most humble country surgeon and the most exalted hospital physician shared a number of assumptions, notably that attendance at medical classes, hospital experience and a qualification were the prerequisites of proper practice. Although there was division over what particular elements a medical education should contain, the broad outlines were rarely contested. All agreed that scientific knowledge was fundamental to sound practice, even though what should constitute that knowledge was subject to great dispute. A basic education in anatomy, physiology and chemistry was deemed essential and hospital-based clinical training in medicine and surgery was seen as imperative. Midwifery too was increasingly regarded as a medical discipline. Demands brought some results. During these years the Society of Apothecaries increasingly extended and tightened up its licensing requirements (Lawrence, S. 1991). By various educational marks, medical men seemed to agree, a properly constituted *profession* should be known, even if it contained men following different medical occupations. It followed, many medical men argued, that this profession should, in some way, be recognized by the state, and given certain privileges. Such claims, however, competed with so many others of a contrary nature and medical men were so divided among themselves as to the way forward, that pleas for protection fell on relatively deaf ears. None the less there were small corporate gains for orthodox medicine in this period, one of the most significant of which was related to the teaching of human anatomy.

Human anatomical dissection in the West can be traced in a continuous tradition to the Renaissance. In the eighteenth century it had increasingly become one of the practices by which orthodox medical men identified themselves. In France, huge overcrowded hospitals seem to have provided surgeons with any number of corpses from a population of sick poor. In Britain things were different. Dissection by the Company of Surgeons was regarded by rich and poor alike as the final indignity to be inflicted on the convicted felon. After hanging, a murderer's body could be taken from the gallows and transported to the surgeons' headquarters for this ultimate degradation. Any suggestion that surgeons were dissecting corpses not so obtained might be met with a riot, the eighteenth-century crowd policing the moral boundaries which surgeons stepped outside at their peril. After about 1790 demand for corpses grew steadily. Students at the hospitals, private schools, the Colleges and the universities increasingly perceived anatomical dissection as a distinguishing characteristic of a medical education. The Colleges of Surgeons in London and in Edinburgh required candidates for their naval surgeon's license to have anatomical knowledge. Anatomy teachers competed for their audiences by providing more and more corpses. The new pathological anatomy was also predicated on post-mortem examination. Some anatomy teachers, not surprisingly, extended their search for corpses beyond legitimate sources. By the 1820s medical demand was outstripping supply and in Edinburgh two local body-snatchers, Burke and Hare, filled the gap with a murder or two. Anatomy teachers and others lobbied parliament to legislate to provide more legitimate subjects. What is noteworthy is that many informed their arguments with utilitarian concerns.[7] They stressed the need for corpses for educational purposes, the importance of rational understanding to medical progress, and the waste of dead bodies which could otherwise be turned to this-worldly use and the benefit of others. After a highly contested campaign during the late 1820s, an Anatomy Act was passed in 1832. The Anatomy Act made available to anatomy teachers unclaimed corpses of the poor dying in hospitals. Dissection, the final stigma of criminality, of the outcast, was transferred to the pauper. This change was not unobserved by contemporaries. The reformers were attacked on just these grounds. Utilitarian thinking, however, had its way. If the poor could not be useful in life, they might at least be so in death (Richardson 1987).

This legal relation between orthodox medicine and the pauper was one of the early legislative signals of an increasingly close involvement of medical men in the lives (and births and deaths) of the poor. As we have noted, orthodox medical contact with the poor before this period was not unknown and during these years the increasingly crowded, fever-ridden towns and cities of the industrial revolution were becoming foci of interest to small numbers of medical men. The stress on small numbers is important here, the overwhelming majority of doctors spent their working lives trying to build or sustain their practices. To a great extent those doctors who did take an interest in disease among the urban poor employed eighteenth-century models which had been developed in institutional contexts. Using this approach, observers emphasized the importance of locality and poverty in the production of sickness in cities. As practical responses, doctors founded or helped found dispensaries and fever hospitals, to which the concerned middle class could also subscribe, where they treated the poor for free (Pickstone 1992). Although some medical men were concerned to describe the fevers and the conditions which seemingly generated them in industrial towns, there were few possibilities within British parochial life for medical men to implement either the preventative models they had developed in the Navy or the model of medical police which had been created on the continent. The former depended on the supervision and discipline attainable in closed institutions and the latter on an extensive, centrally directed bureaucracy. Neither of these conditions pertained in the rapidly-expanding slums of industrial cities. Even at the local level medical men had little clout. The 1820s did see a number of medical men compiling statistics and describing industrial diseases but the perception that, if there was anything wrong with British towns, medical knowledge was the key which should be employed to put this right, was one which was shared by scarcely a handful of authors. These perceptions were to change quite markedly.

Perceptions of epidemic disease in the West have always been integrated with perceptions of social disorder. For example, as we saw above, naval surgeons found the origins of scurvy and fever in laziness and indiscipline. For the historian, epidemic disease can reveal the means, both material and ideological, normally used to maintain order. The responses to plague in the seventeenth century, for instance, expose the intricate social machinery and religious beliefs integral to the ordering of early modern society (Slack 1985). They also reveal that there was often not much of a role for medicine in such circumstances. Its place was largely confined to the treatment of the sick individual.

Epidemic disease in the burgeoning towns of industrial England reveals how frail the machinery was which maintained order and sustained it during a crisis. The cholera epidemics reveal this fragility particularly vividly. In 1831–2 Asiatic cholera swept through British towns and cities, predominantly visiting the homes of the poor. Among middle-class ratepayers and in vestries and in parliament, cholera generated a number of responses. Anxiety was expressed that the disease could, as it sometimes did, notably in Scottish towns and cities, spread into more affluent areas. Cholera aroused sincere humanitarian sentiment and religious compassion for the sufferers. But since it visited Britain during a period of severe political unrest, it also aroused serious concern that outbreaks of the disease, deep in densely populated areas, would become the loci of insurrection, the seeds of breakdown of law and order. Cholera, indeed, was associated with rioting, most commonly against medical men. The doctors were held, for example, to be removing corpses of cholera victims for dissection.

Not surprisingly responses to the cholera were overwhelmingly local. Although a Central Board was set up its authority was limited and it laid its main emphasis on the establishment of local boards. These comprised the local ruling class. Medical representation on these boards was often slim but they did sit doctors alongside local élites in an official capacity (and for the first time). The weakness of medical orthodoxy, however, was revealed in the number of instances in which doctors on the boards denied the existence of cholera in response to pressure from mercantile interests opposed to quarantine. (Doctors did not lie, it was possible to see an outbreak of febrile diarrhoea as any one of several disorders.) Local measures included attempts to suppress vagrancy, removal of nuisances, isolation of cases, the creation of temporary hospitals, provision of burial grounds, enactments to curb movements of the sick, the establishment of food kitchens and whitewashing of the homes of the poor (Morris 1976). These actions were usually funded by a local rate and were also sponsored charitably. All these measures, plus the flight of many of the wealthy, reveal how meagre the material resources of local control were (raising money to fund a board's actions was a chronic problem). However widespread rioting aimed at political targets did not occur. Working-class and middle-class reformers were either reluctant or unable to exploit the cholera for political ends. To middle-class radicals promoting parliamentary reform, the cholera seemed to be too unmanageable to be harnessed into their programme (Durey 1979).

Equally interesting as the material responses to the epidemic were the ideological resources which were drawn on in the time of cholera. Of these religion was by far the most important. Religion figured large as a means for explaining, managing and alleviating the disease. In middle-class families, and working-class families where there was religion, prayer could bring comprehension and compensation and, it was hoped, relief. Some regarded cholera as a direct divine intervention, a punishment for wickedness. Others saw it as the natural working out of God's laws. Those who prayed prayed for the sick, for God's help and for the souls of the dead. They prayed too, to thank God when it was all over. Contemporaries specifically noted that clergymen were prominent among those caring for the sick. Compared to this religious response which located and diffused the horrors of cholera, the medical response appears fragmented and incoherent. Medical men could not agree on the cause, the cure or the means of prevention. Was the cause, they asked, in the water or in the air? Did cholera arise from a local conspiracy of circumstances or was it carried by a specific agent? Unlike the clergy, who many agreed had a legitimate role in explaining the works of God to men, society in the age of William IV had no order or caste that was generally acknowledged to be the custodian of the natural knowledge of the causes of health and disease. Those who claimed such custodianship – the doctors – could not agree among themselves.

The first really significant formal involvement of medical men in the lives of the poor came, almost incidently, from an initiative which was not of their own making. The Poor Law Amendment Act of 1834, it is generally agreed, was the product of the craftsmanship of the barrister, Edwin Chadwick (Finer 1952). The legalist, Chadwick, formerly Jeremy Bentham's secretary, discovered in that thinker's philosophy a science of society, utilitarianism, which he applied to what nearly all agreed was an economic waste, poverty itself. Essentially the new Poor Law abolished out-relief for the able-bodied, on the expectation that those truly in need would voluntarily enter a union workhouse.[8] This institution was Chadwick's monument. Besides their quota of the elderly, children and plain unemployed and unemployable, workhouses also sheltered the sick. Gradually, in the biggest of these institutions, infirmaries were created to separate the sick from the relatively hale. To provide attendance in these places, Boards of Guardians were empowered to employ medical men. Guardians also hired doctors – District Medical Officers – to treat the sick poor in their homes, continuing a practice established under the old Poor Law. But this now occurred on an ever increasing scale. These Poor Law positions were both despised and sought after. They were despised for the meagre wages penny-pinching Guardians paid and they were sought after as mere employment in a time of great medical competition. They were positions for the general practitioners. Although they lacked any of the kudos attached to appointments at the great teaching hospitals, they just might introduce the doctor to the local worthies (Hodgkinson 1967).

The historical significance of these positions, however, is far greater than their relation to nineteenth-century parochialism. Despised though they were as individual positions, the fact that Guardians had to appoint 'duly licensed' medical men indicates that orthodoxy had preference (how much is hard to tell) when the establishment chose among the many sorts of medicine on offer. Although appointments were local, ultimately they derived from the orders of the Poor Law Commissioners framed in 1834. Local execution of central orders had been typical of English government since at least the sixteenth century, but in this instance central authority had conceded medicine an instrumental value in the everyday running of society.

In one way or another the new Poor Law was to be the principal means by which medicine was harnessed into the running of nineteenth-century society. Not long after its passage it was manifest to all that the Poor Law Amendment Act had not solved the problem of poverty. In a report of 1832 Chadwick had taken little notice of any relation between poverty and disease. By the late 1830s he perceived their relationship to be the crucial factor underlying the failure of the new Poor Law to work with thorough efficiency (the link was, of course, visible to many others besides Chadwick). Chadwick attacked this issue in the same way he had addressed Poor Law reform, by applying science to society. In this instance he turned to the new science of social reform, statistics (the tool of the 'statist', the student of the state). The statistical movement flourished in the 1830s, notably stimulated by actuarial work.[9] Chadwick measured disease and disorder by compiling returns of statistics from Poor Law officers and others throughout the kingdom. The result was his famous *Report on the Sanitary Condition of the Labouring Population* of 1842. The *Report* repeatedly made the case that disease among the poor was a major cause of economic waste. In particular disease was cited as the cause of the failure of the new Poor Law to function as it should. Although the *Report* was widely regarded as the achievement of one man, it is important to see the consensus which sustained Chadwick's initiative and conclusions.

As we have noted, for the most part, doctors were not particularly active in bringing a unique medical perspective to bear on the disorder of the industrial city. Most practitioners gave their time solely to private work. The perspective of medical men was not that of a professional group but distributed in much the same way as the perspective of the middle- and lower middle-class population as a whole. Where we do find medical men studying the slum and the factory, it is primarily as middle-class reformers rather than as members of a medical profession. Thus they might be, for example, first and foremost Benthamites or evangelicals who happened to deploy medical understanding in the cause of political or moral reform. The results of their careful local research were polemical texts, not simply compilations of statistics for medical consumption. Thus the physician James Kay's (later Kay-Shuttleworth) study of the Manchester slums of 1832 was entitled, *The Moral and Physical Condition of the Working Classes*.

In the 1820s and 1830s and increasingly in the 1840s, a small number of medical men busied themselves with the disorders of civic life. They included general practitioners active in local statistical societies, or working as District Medical Officers, compiling data on disease and disorder in their towns and boroughs. Some of them belonged to their local phrenological association. Some were active in the cause of medical reform. Some of these statisticians are quite well known, for instance, John Hutchinson. In Hutchinson's work we can see how industrial society fostered the gradual creation and application of a new, medical, concept of normality. A surgeon and an active statistician, Hutchinson had an appointment with the Britannia Life Assurance Company. He devised an instrument, the spirometer, for estimating the amount of air flowing into and out of the lung. Hutchinson described his uses of this instrument at a meeting of the Statistical Society in 1844. Using this device on large samples of the population he drew up tables from which he created statistical categories of normality and abnormality of lung function (Spriggs 1977). The significance of this goes far beyond the invention of a medical test.

To a great extent England in the eighteenth century had been a face-to-face society. People were known and made their way in the world by and through their personal connections. To be known in this way was to be subject to various obligations and these were the ties that bound eighteenth-century society together. Personal knowledge was social control. Although this generally held true, gradually a number of men, notably medical men, were building another way of knowing. The instrument of this new knowledge was statistics (Tröhler 1979). During the industrial revolution and after, many areas of life were run in the eighteenth-century manner, but it seemed clear to some that it was impossible that a large population, living in a working-class slum, for instance, could be known in this traditional fashion and thus controlled in the traditional way. Building on the work of eighteenth-century enquirers they insisted that there must be natural laws governing (and that was their word) the behaviour of such populations (Pickstone 1984). When such laws were known, they said, populations could be properly managed. Hutchinson's work illustrates one aspect of this shifting perception. Hutchinson's life tables for the insurance companies and his spirometer readings were tools for describing the population as a whole, for constituting the normal but also for situating each individual in relation to it. Advantages of birth and patronage continued to count for a great deal in Victorian society but it was also, increasingly, a world in which discrimination and selection were based on measurement, whether it was a written *examination* for the civil service or a physical *examination* for life insurance (Ginzburg 1980).

This revolution did not come from within medicine. It was not generated autonomously by that increasing self-conscious body of men who were beginning to think of themselves as constituting a medical profession. But medicine was one of the modes of rational enquiry that was fundamental to effecting the transformation. Doctors, after all, dealt with the basic stuff out of which societies are made – men's and women's bodies – and they made those bodies into the sorts of objects of knowledge that helped to make it possible for Victorian industrial society to function in the way that it did. A move to precision, universalism, and standardization characterized Victorian medicine just as it did the factory, the railways, the clock and the coinage.

Rational medicine in the eighteenth century had a language for constituting a person in terms of his life history and experiences. It could describe a person's own *natural* state and (sometimes) restore him to it if he fell sick. Nineteenth-century medical men were developing a language (which we still use) for situating all people in relation to each other, for measuring their deviation from the *normal*, and, increasingly, for managing their deviations from that norm.[10] The normal was in turn regarded as the expression of a natural law. This gradual embedding of medicine and statistics in the fabric of nineteenth-century life is nowhere more evident than in the establishment of the General Register Office in 1837. Here were recorded national statistics on births, deaths and causes of death (this latter requirement was Chadwick's doing). Significantly the Compiler of Abstracts at the office was a doctor, William Farr, who for forty years used the statistical returns to investigate the geography of mortality in Victorian towns (Eyler 1979).

Thus Chadwick's work in the late 1830s, the 1840s and beyond, was sustained by the view that essential to the management of civil society was the collection and employment of statistics. Statistics revealed natural law and could suggest action in accord with it. Many reformers held such views, including a few doctors. One of these, prominent in Chadwick's own circle, was Thomas Southwood Smith, also a Benthamite. Smith contributed to the Poor Law Commission's work of 1838, reporting on sickness among the poor in London's Bethnal Green and Whitechapel. Other physicians who figured among Chadwick's allies were James Kay and Neil Arnott who had made names for themselves in the statistics movement. Kay was an assistant Poor Law Commissioner who, in 1838, with Arnott, produced a report for the Commission on fever in London. Arnott was a friend of Bentham and another utilitarian, the young John Stuart Mill. During the 1840s the voices of these men were part of a network which increasingly called for what was now being designated 'sanitary reform'.

Sanitary reform sounds so rational today that it is hard to see how in the 1830s and 1840s it was a perceived by many to be a partisan solution to what was also seen as a partisan problem. To a great extent, many sanitary reformers saw the new Poor Law as the correct or scientific solution to the problem of poverty.[11] It was correct because it was viewed as legislation enacted in accord with natural laws. For instance, one of these natural laws dictated an inevitable relation between population increase and misery. This 'law' had been described by the Reverend Thomas Malthus in his *Essay on Population* of 1798. Malthus's work was interpreted by many to mean that out-door poor relief simply pauperized and demoralized the poor further. It protected them from the operation of natural law. The relative prosperity conferred by relief encouraged them to have children and in the end their misery was compounded.[12] But all agreed that the new Poor Law, however correct in principle it seemed, had manifestly failed to solve the problem of poverty. Reformers thus sought for what they saw as poverty's residual causes. They directed their attentions to identifying those features of the lives of the poor which, they said, unlike economic forces, were open to legislative manipulation. Many of the poor, they found, could not work because of sickness, notably fever. Fever reduced the able-bodied to pauperism; thus fever in the slum went some way to explaining the failure of the new Poor Law. This was, to a great extent, an inversion of an eighteenth-century view which accounted what were held as the consequences of poverty itself – uncleanliness, overcrowding, poor diet, immorality – to be the main causes of fever. Having found the origins of poverty in fever, sanitary reformers turned to the immediate causes of fever, or at least those causes which seemed amenable to political action. These they found in the emanations from drains, cesspools, refuse pits and burial grounds (Pickstone 1992). 'Atmospheric impurity' was the prime cause of fever (Chadwick 1965, 75). Accounts of how this cause operated varied, but in one version local decomposition of animal matter produced poisons which set up similar decomposition in the victim's body. Poisoning, rather than person-to-person transmission (contagion) was the model employed by the sanitarians (Ackerknecht 1948; Cooter 1982). Such a model fitted neatly with free-trade, anti-quarantine sentiments.

It is noteworthy that many of the medical men involved in sanitary reform were Dissenters, provincials, men with minor hospital appointments: not members of the élite and not the humblest general practitioners. They were also among the men who were importing the new, French, local pathology and physical examination into British medicine. Many of them were active in seeking the pathology of fever by means of post-mortem examination. Just as, in one sense, the new clinical medicine made the patient less important than the disease, so too the sanitarian view rendered the fever patient merely a body in physical and chemical decay (Pickstone 1992). By defining the problems of fever and poverty in these ways, sanitarians framed their solutions in professional and legislative terms rather than in terms of face-to-face contact or in terms which challenged the economic fabric of Victorian society. In many ways then, the problem of fever among the poor was not, for the sanitarians, medical, nor was the solution.

Others saw things differently. A number of medical men, such as the Edinburgh professor, William Pultney Alison, rejected this approach and continued to find the causes of fever in the consequences of poverty: diet, overcrowding and moral laxity. Many Tories and evangelicals saw the problem of poverty and fever as the failure of paternalism. In turn they rejected any suggestion of centrally orchestrated reform. Radicals, too, saw central intervention as interference, removing control of public expenditure from local authorities. For many, the problem of the poor was *primarily* of moral or religious origin and required an appropriate solution. The cholera of 1832, remember, had been perceived by many as having its roots in moral or religious failure. Sanitary reform was a partisan solution in another way. In so far as reformers proposed legislation, they were proposing a new relation between a central state and its subjects. Many radicals and Tories regarded such legislative intervention with deep suspicion (Smith, F.B. 1979).

Agitation for sanitary reform grew in the 1840s, especially after Chadwick's *Report*. This massive catalogue of the material world in which the poor lived and of the incidence of disease and death among them drew attention to the economic cost of fever in towns. The report also took notice of the habits of the poor. It observed that the conditions in which the poor lived were the source of their immorality, noting that 'adverse circumstances tend to produce an adult population short-lived, improvident, restless, and intemperate, and with habitual avidity for sensual gratifications' (Chadwick 1965, 423). This was a conclusion not universally shared, for some saw poverty as a consequence of a failure to be thrifty and industrious. Compared to Chartism, the Anti-Corn Law League and the ten hours' agitation, the sanitary reform movement had a low profile. It was almost entirely a middle-class movement and limited to a fraction of the class at that. Its significance is not to be measured by its limited visibility, however, but in terms of the sorts of solution it was offering to the condition of a new, industrial society.

The sanitary reform campaigns of the 1840s proceeded at the local level and through central lobbying. Local organizations were formed, in which doctors might or might not be prominent. Committees, commissions, associations and societies produced surveys and reports. In many of these things Chadwick and others of the Benthamite persuasion were active. Their reward was the Public Health Act of 1848. The significance of this Act scarcely lies in its content. It was for the most part permissive, empowering local authorities, if they wished, to initiate local reforms for removing nuisances, laying down sewers and so forth. But, as a government intervention into the conditions perceived to be connected with the production of disease, it was monumental. It was another significant turning point for medical men too. The Act made provision for towns to appoint a medical officer of health (MOH) and was interpreted as requiring such men to have an orthodox medical qualification. The MOH was to be responsible for local inspection and compilation of statistics. These men were watchdogs of the Act rather than executives with the power to initiate action independent of local authorities. None the less, the posts were a triumph for the doctors, since, however lowly such appointment might seem, they represented further recognition of orthodoxy. Although what special skills a medical man could bring to bear when dealing with overcrowded cellars, polluted water or overflowing cesspits, does not seem to have been an issue. Engineers or civil servants, however, might have been equally appropriate appointees.

Ironically 1848 saw the return of cholera. It reappeared again in 1853-4. Both epidemics swept through the slums and, once again, the disorder they produced was cause for alarm. Preventative and curative measures seemed as ineffectual as they did in 1832. None the less, compared to 1832, there were subtle differences in the responses to these later epidemics. To begin with, neither of them was associated with the degree of rioting, and especially rioting against medical men, that was experienced in the 1832 epidemic. The second difference can be spotted in the answer of the Home Secretary, Lord Palmerston, in 1853, to requests by church groups for the declaration of a day of fasting. Palmerston replied that, in the absence of the eradication of contagion, prayer was fruitless (Durey 1979). Later, medical men detected in this statement a definite change of national tone, the suggestion of a move from religious to scientific authority. Not that the doctors could agree on the cause of cholera, on whether it was locally generated or transmitted by the same sort of agent on every occasion. None the less, there had been subtle changes in the medical approach to cholera since the 1832 epidemic. These changes are a measure of how some medical men were attempting to create an autonomous *medical* science as an investigative tool and solution to the problem of disorder. Chadwick's approach was informed by the view that cholera was locally generated, associated with filth and nuisance and that an organized engineering solution (based on water supply and sewage removal) would prevent the problem in future. But in London, doctors like John Snow and William Farr, and in Bristol, William Budd, were carrying out epidemiological enquiries, and complementing these studies with microscopical investigation and animal experiments (Pelling 1978).

Chadwick had little or no time for the pathological and aetiological aspects of these enquiries and it is important to see the cultural shift occurring here. Fevers in general, and cholera in particular, were areas of contest where minorities struggled to achieve social and cultural supremacy through recognition of the validity of their claims to be able to explain and control disorder. The resources such groups used to underwrite these claims varied. Those of the church are obvious. Because they laid claim to be the legitimate interpreters of acts of God, the various churches spoke loudly in the cholera years. It would be wrong, however, to see in Palmerston's answer a significant decline in theological authority and a massive rise in scientific credibility between the 1832 and 1854 epidemics, and for two reasons. First there was not one science of disorder but many. The one most prominent in the 1830s and 1840s was utilitarianism. This was the science of the legislator and, in Chadwick's interpretation of it, medical men had the role of humble fact gatherers. Medical accounts of the pathological processes constituting disease were deemed (at least by Chadwick) to be of marginal importance. Engineering, the construction of sewers and the supply of water were more important to such sanitarians than medical measures. But by 1854, in the work of Snow, Budd, Farr and others, we begin to see the creation of a new *medical* science of disorder, the promotion of medically informed solutions and the advancement of the claims of the medical expert. Within this science, detailed knowledge of the biology, pathology and epidemiology of disease were deemed the foundations of action.

For the second reason why we should not look for conflict between medical science and religion within this period we must turn to the clerics and doctors themselves. Many clergymen were keen promoters of the study of nature and a great number of doctors were devout. Both groups shared a belief in a moral universe in which nature's laws were one of the ways through which man could discern God's providence. For example, although fever and cholera might seem monstrous contradictions of God's provisions for mankind, examples of a world turned upside-down, from another perspective they were simply failures of those normal provisions. Thus, many doctors and clerics shared the view that God had created a nature which was permeated with cycles of degeneration and growth, decay and rebirth. Processes such as putrefaction, the decay of animal and vegetable products, were seen by Victorians as part of the divine provision for life (Hamlin 1985). The symptoms of disease, especially febrile disease, were commonly viewed by doctors and others as arising from a putrefactive process in the body. Disease was part of the normal cycle of nature occurring in the wrong place. Such an assumption provided the foundations of clinical and epidemiological investigations of fever as well as the basis for prescriptive moral doctrines; discourses on how society and the life of the individual should be ordered.

We have seen how, by about 1850, orthodox medicine was being employed to facilitate the running of Victorian society. There was one further area where we can observe this employment on a relatively substantial scale: in the management of madness. In turn we can see that medical men, by their creation and deployment of sciences of the mind, were both developing concepts of the normal and discriminating more finely among the population. Doctors, by employing naturalistic theories of mental disturbance, had long claimed the prerogative of defining and treating madness. Such claims, however, were often contested or only partially acknowledged. In the seventeenth century, even when it was agreed that a sufferer's body was disturbed, madness could regularly be put down to witchcraft, devilment or an act of God. During the Enlightenment, the naturalism which, to a large extent, was sustained and given its detail by medical men, increasingly prevailed when the mad took centre stage. We can see this clearly in coroners' courts' verdicts on suicide. In the seventeenth century it was not uncommon for courts to find the origin of this act in a supernatural agency. In the eighteenth century, the fault was increasingly designated as lying in madness from natural causes (MacDonald and Murphy 1990).

Enlightenment medical men theorized about madness and increasingly implicated the nervous system as having some part in the derangement. This system, too, they found primarily at fault in lesser disorders in which the mind was affected: melancholia, hysteria and hypochondriasis. Recognition that doctors had some expertise with regard to the mad had been given in a number of ways in the eighteenth-century; for example, in a parliamentary act of 1774 by which members of the College of Physicians were appointed to inspect madhouses in London. In the case of the madness of George III, orthodox medicine's claim to have the means to control the deranged were made very public. Yet, for the most part, madness remained beyond the cares or control of medical men. Many of the mad poor still roamed free or were confined at home or in the local workhouse. Private madhouses, where the wealthy incarcerated their troublesome relatives and where, at the expense of the parish, the mad poor might be detained were quite common. But although doctors were often the proprietors or attendants at such places they were not medical institutions.

Systematically distinguishing each of the mad from the sane, discriminating among the mad themselves by defining their disorder, and segregating them in special institutions were practices foreign to the workings of eighteenth-century society. But that society did provide the intellectual and material inheritance from which these things could be elaborated. As in so many areas, nineteenth-century reformers took over eighteenth-century ideas and institutions and moulded them to new ends.

Specialized public institutions for the confinement of the mad were not unknown in the eighteenth century. Some, such as the medieval hospital, Bethlem, the eighteenth century had itself inherited. A few charitable 'lunatic hospitals' were also established in the Enlightenment, notably the Asylum at York, founded in 1777, which became notorious for secrecy and maltreatment of its inmates (Porter, R. 1987). By the beginning of the nineteenth-century, evangelical instincts and Benthamite reforming sentiments had begun to sniff out public asylums and proliferating private madhouses as seats of gross abuse. There were eighteenth-century institutions devoted to the compassionate care of the mad, but these, such as the Retreat, founded by the Society of Friends in York in 1792, were religious places rather than medical ones. For the most part the care of lunatics was custodial and neither predominantly medical nor religious and cataloguing its grossest abuses was easy enough. What is interesting to the historian surveying the reform movement from the perspective of medicine are two things. First, that reform took the direction of increasing segregation and confinement of all the mad. Second, that custodianship was entrusted more frequently to medical men. These two things were, of course, intimately related.

Various parliamentary acts between 1808 and 1845 enabled and then required the establishment of county lunatic asylums, paid for from the rates, for the incarceration of the mad poor. The massive asylum at Hanwell, Middlesex, was perhaps the most famous of these. The requirements of medical attendance and inspection were also gradually tightened. Institutional segregation of all the mad was part of the general nineteenth-century move to institutionalization and specialist management, variously driven by evangelicalism, paternalism and efficiency (Hilton 1988). The workhouse, the hospital, the school, the factory, the prison and the asylum all segregated, distinguished among, and controlled the poor by institutional means. In all of these instances, to a greater or lesser extent, orthodox medicine was a source of rationalization: the body of knowledge which explained why this was the best way to do things. Medical men were the body of practitioners who on a day-to-day basis acted, either directly or indirectly, for the good (as it had been defined) of those they cared for. There was nothing inexorable about this. Reform *could* have taken the form of decarceration, asylums *might* have become primarily religious institutions. It happened the way it did because those who finally prevailed in Victorian society viewed institutionalization as the rational way to proceed. Asylums became medical institutions because medical men increasingly claimed technical competence to explain and control madness and the public increasingly listened to them (Scull 1979). Medical men also cleaned up their own act. They hunted out doctors who flagrantly milked the private madhouses. Texts on the neurological basis of lunacy or insanity (rather than madness) proliferated in the 1820s and 1830s. Medical men scaled down their recommendations for physical treatment and began to insist on the moral relations of insanity (adopting ideas and techniques from religious institutions such as the York Retreat). As in the case of the sane, discipline, industry and devotion were held to work wonders. The science of the alienists (or psychiatrists as they became) endorsed the morality of middle-class reform. Victorian society increasingly listened to the views of the expert who claimed authority on the basis of scientific knowledge. When, during the early nineteenth century, coal mines became so deep that the loss of life became a scandal, the solution was for a chemist, Sir Humphry Davy, to devise a safety lamp, not to question whether men and women should labour in this way (Berman 1978). In the case of asylums, medical authority was not easily achieved and when it was it hardly brought the doctor much kudos. None the less, in the first half of the nineteenth century a small number of orthodox medical men had deliberately shaped themselves as experts in the diagnosis and management of the mad, and used the most up-to-date science, initially phrenology, to do so. By the mid-century the 'mad doctor', along with the MOH and the Poor Law medical officer, was almost a respectable figure.

3 Modernity

In 1858 a parliamentary act required the creation of a medical register. This effectively recognized a distinct medical profession in Britain. The Act did not debar unqualified persons from practising, but it did distinguish them as different from men with registerable qualifications. At first sight such legislation is surprising. After all, it was a piece of outright protectionism passed during the summer of Victorian liberalism. Freedom to practise medicine in whatever way one wished, without any legal interference, was regarded in some places as a fundamental human right or liberty. It had been seen that way in France during the Revolution when, briefly, all privileged medical institutions had been abolished. It was very much seen that way in the United States where regulars competed on absolutely equal legal terms with every other sort of practitioner. It was, indeed, viewed that way by many people in Britain. Adam Smith, the prophet of liberalism for the Victorians, had argued that even the awarding of medical degrees amounted to unfair advantage. The opponents of the Medical Act saw it that way too. Nevertheless, the regulars won the day. Why was this so? By the 1850s, orthodox medicine had become a significant feature of the machinery of the Victorian state. Even though homeopaths treated the nobility and even royalty, alternative systems had not gained even the smallest amount of official recognition. Indeed, Poor Law doctors who used homeopathic remedies were the subject of inquisitions by Boards of Guardians (Hodgkinson 1967, 337). Regularly qualified men oiled many of the wheels of the state. Even though most employment was at the local level, it nearly all derived from central initiatives and nearly all of it involved the poor. By the late 1850s, medical men could work either part or full time as, for example, factory medical inspectors, prison doctors, medical officers of health, Poor Law medical officers and vaccinators, often holding more than one position simultaneously. The army and the Royal Navy, of course, still offered full-time careers.

Surveying the growth of Victorian central government from a distance, the 1858 Act was a recognition, in law, of this relationship between orthodox practice and the state. The Act, as the 1815 Apothecaries' Act had been, was largely the consequence of agitation from below. Hundreds of medical men struggling in private practice and public employment to attain respectability and security campaigned for a single, state-recognized profession. As in the case of the 1815 Act, they got few of the things for which they had battled. The most radical reformers wanted a single profession, a single system of medical education and a single qualification. They got a single profession, in the form of the medical register, with a General Medical Council (GMC) to oversee it. But the patchwork of education and the variety of qualifications remained untouched. The Royal Colleges, the metropolitan hospitals and their medical schools and the ancient and new universities, had impressive local and national influence and were scarcely going to simply sit and watch their privileges be nullified. Much of the power of the medical élite was seated in the council rooms of the great colleges. It was used to keep at bay the rank-and-file. Few were prepared to renounce any control and unite around a single qualification. Indeed, the most powerful parties, unsurprisingly, sought to add to that which they already possessed. In these senses then, the Act was a triumph for the élites.

Yet, looked at from another perspective, the fact that any act was passed at all has a slightly remarkable quality. In the enactment we seem to be watching something very general about Victorian Britain and something very particular about medicine. The general phenomenon is that of profession formation, in which the interests of previously disparate, possibly antagonistic, occupational groups are to some extent pooled, and a claim to unity predominates in public situations. Attempts to achieve this pooling characterize much early nineteenth-century medical agitation. The *Medical Directory*, a compilation of orthodox practitioners, was first published in 1845. It would serve, declared its editors, 'to promote union amongst all grades of the profession' (Dupree and Crowther 1991). The unity which some medical men claimed they had achieved around the mid-nineteenth century was based, they said, on their broadly similar educational background and shared scientific expertise. Yet this general perspective does not catch the particular features of the change. For if the profession had a public face of unity, it still had a private one of division and élitism. Power in medicine, as measured by income and local or national political influence, remained securely with the few. Indeed, in spite of reform it is arguable that this power was greater than ever before. The ideological conflicts over scientific knowledge which had been an aspect of the agitation in the 1830s had all but disappeared. Private medical schools were going out of business and the generation and transmission of knowledge was fairly safely in the hands of the Colleges, the universities and the great hospitals. It was the disappearance of the cognitive dimension to intramedical conflict which made possible, on occasion, the show of unity. But within, the organization of medicine was denounced by the rank-and-file as undemocratic. In the institutions associated with the élite, notably the great hospitals, nepotism and patronage figured large in promotion and professional progress. When appointments were made to senior posts, governors looked for gentlemen and men who were politically safe. The great physicians and surgeons ensured junior positions went to their relatives and friends (Peterson 1978).

The few then never really lost control of medicine, as is evidenced by the fact that, throughout the century, the rank-and-file saw it as important to focus their reforming energies on the institutional bases of the élite. But the élite was much more secure by the 1860s. What is remarkable here is the story of the continuity behind the radical upheaval of the 1830s and 1840s. By the 1860s and 1870s the culture (but not the social place) of élite medicine was, in many ways, quite different from that of forty years earlier, yet it was still seamlessly part of high culture generally. In this respect the history of the continuity of the medical élite is the history of how they transformed themselves in line with the rest of the Victorian establishment. The naturalization of mind provides an elegant example of the persisting *political* place but changing culture of this élite.

As we have observed, during the first half of the nineteenth century, rank-and-file doctors pressed for reform. In many instances they supported the legitimacy of their case by recourse to new accounts of the natural world. Many of these accounts were radical and materialist, denying the existence of the soul (or a non-material mind) and thus the authority and role of the church. One of the most striking and popular of these accounts was phrenology. Phrenology did not necessarily entail denial of the existence of the soul, but in the hands of many of its protagonists it was shaped into a radical philosophy in which the operations of the mind were divided into the labours of different parts of the brain. The phrenologists situated mind within nature, in the same way that Malthus had said social phenomena, notably poverty, were comprehensible in terms of natural law. Malthus's account of natural law was employed to reactionary ends – to deny the value of out-door relief. For phrenologists, however, the naturalization of mind was used to advocate democratic reform. The general point is that industrial society saw increasing recourse to naturalistic legitimations of change across the political spectrum. Nature was increasingly pointed to as a source of authority for resolving political issues. In the case of establishment authors, God was deemed to have created a nature whose moral lessons expanded, or at least did not contradict, those of the Bible. In the instance of many reformers, nature itself was held to be a sufficient source of morals.

Doctors of all political persuasions were significant figures in the creation of this ideology of naturalism. Thus we find, early in the century, élite medical men in the corporations, the great hospitals and the universities enjoining and joining in scientific enquiry – the study of natural phenomena. As regards the nervous system and the brain, however, members of the medical élite, with one or two exceptions, were unanimous in their condemnation of what they perceived as dangerous doctrines, such as phrenology. The brain, they said, was the seat of the soul or mind and this was not amenable to physiological and experimental analysis. Man and animal, they declared, were irrevocably different. Yet, in fact, over the period 1820–70 the human brain and spinal cord were increasingly viewed by medical men *of all persuasions* as containing nothing other than very complex elaborations of the organizational and functional elements that they described as characterizing the nervous systems of animals. By the 1870s, orthodox medical men, many of them distinguished practitioners, had created a new naturalistic account of mind, in which the brain was experimentally investigated and designated as the organ of divided mental labour (Young 1990). This doctrine was not that of the once hated, and now ridiculed phrenologists. But the casual observer might be forgiven for seeing a similarity. The new doctrine was proclaimed to be based on legitimate physiological enquiry. Its thoroughgoing naturalism was completed by linking it to evolutionism, notably by using Darwin's theory of natural selection. Mind was the outcome of gradual change in nature. This account of mind, of 'man's place in nature' as it was called, was, in its details, unlike phrenology. Yet in its overall naturalism it was virtually identical. The important point is that the social relations in which it was embedded were quite different. Whereas phrenology was the naturalism of outsiders, of radical reformers, this new naturalism was, or was becoming, the culture of the Victorian élite. Its creators were respectable doctors, philosophers and natural historians such as T.H. Huxley, Charles Darwin, Herbert Spencer and John Hughlings Jackson. Such naturalism was not a doctrine of reform and revolution, but the new legitimation of stability. Gradual natural progress had brought about the current state of affairs and gradual natural progress would ensure that the future was better than the past. Such naturalism of course did not have a completely easy passage into Victorian culture. Witness the reaction to Darwin's views. None the less, as this instance shows, the medical élite transformed itself, along with the élite of Victorian society. It remained politically on top while aspects of its culture looked quite different from earlier in the century.

In all sorts of detail the new naturalism differed from the old. For instance, one of its most striking features was, particularly towards the end of the century, the claims made for its truth by virtue of one of its methods of enquiry. Animal experimentation had long been regarded by many doctors as a valuable adjunct to scientific investigation. In the 1860s and 1870s, however, descriptions of this practice were gradually elaborated and these credited it with being a method capable of producing knowledge of an unprecedented sort about the body's activities. The modern science of experimental physiology was first shaped on the continent, slowly adopted in Britain in the 1860s (first at University College London and then at Cambridge) and eventually given centrality, not just in the medical curriculum but in the pantheon of the new biological sciences (Geison 1978). This movement was not without resistance. Among medical men some still favoured anatomy and natural history as the key to bodily mysteries. On the wards of the more conservative hospitals, some of the great gentlemen physicians saw it as an incursion by basic scientists (which it was) into a curriculum which they said should rest on a sizeable chunk of classical learning (Lawrence, C. 1985b). Most vigorous of all, however, was the concerted opposition which denied that this was an appropriate means by which human understanding should be enhanced. Antivivisectionism was a formidable movement. Its organizations drew support from nearly all sections of Victorian society. Women were particularly prominent members of the antivivisection groups which campaigned vigorously against experimental medicine in the 1860s and 1870s (Elston 1987). The movement drew on a variety of sentiments and ideologies, notably the view that man was the steward of the animal kingdom and that he had no right to use animals experimentally. The physiologists replied that since medical therapies might come from the practice and since these were, they said, indisputably good, such experimentation was justified. The protagonists argued from utterly different and irreconcilable premises (French 1975). But this was more than just an argument about experimentation on animals. It was a political controversy, conducted in the terms of scientific culture, about who should determine what knowledge was, how it was to be produced and what value society should attach to it. Seen in these wider terms the 1876 Cruelty to Animals Act was a total victory for the new culture of élite medicine. Although the Act licensed and limited animal experimentation, it was an endorsement of the new naturalism.

The decades after the mid-nineteenth century witnessed the medical profession, especially its élite, consolidate its position as a significant order in Victorian society. It did this in a number of ways, two of which we have noted. First, as a social group it was increasingly implicated in the normal running and ordering of society. Second, as we have also observed, through its embrace of naturalism, it was an important creator of Victorian culture. These, the social and cultural relations of medicine, were of course different sides of the same coin. Take the question of medicine and women which neatly illustrates this point.

It is a notable feature of eighteenth- and nineteenth-century natural history that its practitioners (many of them medical men) increasingly perceived sexual difference as a fundamental distinction within nature. Thus Linnaeus's famous botanical system, produced in the mid-eighteenth century, was based on his view that plants reproduced sexually and that the form and number of the reproductive organs could be used as basic facts of botanical classification. Increasingly, the form and function of all parts of plants and animals were held to be related to reproductive differences (Schiebinger 1991). Thus, for example, by 1800, anatomists had discerned a large number of differences between male and female skeletons. Slightly later, phrenologists found marked variations between male and female brains and skulls. Various authors increasingly catalogued what were construed as fundamental behavioral differences between men and women. Thus women were passive, men active; women emotional, men intellectual; women domestic, men outgoing and so on. These distinctions were viewed as elaborations of a basic, sexually-grounded difference. This difference was seen to have provided the natural basis of differing social roles. Woman's nature and thus her natural social role were rooted in her reproductive system (Jordanova 1989). In fact doctors in the nineteenth century created a whole specialized science of the female reproductive system – gynaecology. The practice of gynaecology was not always viewed with approval by the Victorian medical élite who valued generalism as a gentlemanly ideal over specialism. The cultural assumptions on which gynaecology was based, however, were shared with a few exceptions (usually female) by all literate Victorians. The language and practice of gynaecology demonstrated to Victorians, on a day-to-day basis, the enormous determining power of the female reproductive parts. From this determinism flowed naturalistic prescriptions which defined the role of middle-class women in Victorian society. Women who revolted against that role were deemed to have gone against their nature, perhaps involuntarily, through a disorder of their reproductive physiology (Moscucci 1990). Medicine, when defining and demonstrating *normality* through the everyday workings of medical practice, was a much more significant constructor of the Victorian world than when it had an overt policing role, a role greatly disliked by many medical men for ethical, professional and political reasons.

Such overt policing exercises were prescribed in the Contagious Diseases Acts of 1864 and 1866. These Acts were framed with the aim of maintaining order at garrison and dockyard towns. They gave medical men the power to examine prostitutes and, if diseased, keep them confined for up to three months. The Acts provoked great hostility. The opposition included many women, famously Josephine Butler, who denounced the Acts for stigmatizing women and regarding the men who visited prostitutes as blameless. Although there was a powerful medical lobby which viewed the Acts as progressive extensions of public health legislation, many doctors considered them a gross infringement of individual rights (McHugh 1980). The significance of the Acts for us lies in the light which they shed on government trust of orthodox medicine and the preparedness to use it to maintain order in dangerous areas where the normal mechanisms of social control seemed not to be working.[1]

By the 1860s, medical men were not only employed as practitioners by virtue of central government acts, a very small number worked in central government itself. Under the wing of the Privy Council, John Simon, formerly the medical officer of health for the City of London, held an appointment which effectively made him overseer of public health administration. The detailed workings of Simon's department need not concern us here but it is salient to observe how the sanitary reformers, notably Chadwick, had been squeezed out and the professionals had eased themselves in. Simon's approach was different to Chadwick's. Under the auspices of his office basic physiological research was conducted, vaccination was promoted and detailed epidemiological surveys carried out. The latter were employed both to monitor current administration and to form the basis of ongoing piecemeal legislation (Lambert 1963). It is important to see what had happened here. Twenty years earlier sanitary reform had been a contentious issue. Its promoters, notably Chadwick, did not construe it as a medical imperative. If anything, it fell, for many of them, under the rubric of economic rationalization. By the 1860s sanitary reform and administration were being considered a branch of government activity to be handled by medical men.[2] The meaning of sanitary reform was being changed. Once a publicly orchestrated attack on the straightforwardly malodorous, it was becoming a field of expertise in which the causes of disease were deemed detectable only by the microscope or a chemical test.

The social reorganization that had created what was, effectively, a government department of health administration run by medical men was an indicator of a gradual shift in cultural assumptions. The health of the population was still regarded as a key to national prosperity, but increasingly health was being promoted by attending to disease or potential disease, by medically defined means, in individuals.[3] Perhaps for the first time in history, measurable value was being placed on the health of each and every citizen in a society. But, at the same time, how health was to be arrived at, recognized, and, more important, what it was *for*, were being construed in terms of medical intervention. This might be said to be an account of health characteristic of modern industrial societies.

If we look back to the eighteenth century, the health of the population as a whole, if it was reflected on at all, was usually described in terms of national wealth. The promotion and policing of health were equated with mercantile power and economic success. A large and healthy population meant a powerful state. But if we look away from populations to the meanings of individual health, they are to be found in the realm of citizenship and religion. *Mens sana in corpore sano*, a healthy mind in a healthy body, with the implication that they were related, was an ancient maxim that, for the eighteenth century, entailed a moral responsibility. The maintenance of health was essential to the practice of civic virtue. Those qualified to play a part in civic life had a responsibility to follow a healthy regimen. The eighteenth-century debate on luxury brings this point out well: when luxury corrupts, both mind and body are necessarily affected. Health was *for* something. If this meaning of health was for the wealthy, Christian meanings applied to rich and poor. God's laws taught the way to live a healthy life and the Christian had a duty to observe them. Health and virtue were ideally one. Even when sickness was not the fault of the sufferer, disease could still remind him of his mortal state. There were moral lessons to be learnt from sickness whether self-inflicted (and thus a sign of transgression) or whether it came through no fault of one's own.

Throughout the nineteenth century, epidemic disease and individual sickness remained loaded with moral and religious meanings. The signs of syphilis, for instance, were still seen as the stigma of moral turpitude, fever was an indication of self-neglect. None the less, slowly but surely the meanings of health and disease were changed and morally altered. As the body was transformed into a biological object, it became possible to construe, say, pain as no more than an evolved physiological mechanism, and an outbreak of fever as simply the parasitic success of some as yet unknown yeast or germ. In this sense medicine was central to a number of transformations occurring in Victorian culture. A significant instance of this transformation is seen in the history of surgery.

Eighteenth-century élite medicine embodied an ideal of practice as the management of the body. This was a model which, in various forms, can be traced in the practice of quite humble practitioners. The surgical model of disease was rather different and translated into practice more rarely. Mechanically fixing or removing a disorder – a broken bone, a cancerous breast, a bladder stone – was not a procedure to be entered into lightly. The surgeon's model was an artificer's model, a mechanic's approach. As we have noted, the late eighteenth century saw the increasing rise to prominence of the surgeon and with it the surgical point of view. A number of factors conspired to make this possible; first, a positive valuation of practical arts by Enlightenment thinkers and the attempt to base those arts on rational principles (the great *Encyclopédie* of Enlightenment France contains a long, approving article on surgery); second, the rise of a medicine of populations, to which surgical-like models of specific disease were applied; and third, the increasingly successful employment of hospitals by surgeons as their institutional base. In France in particular it was in the hospitals that surgeons began to extend their view of disease. Here pathological changes of the interior of the body were increasingly seen as local tissue changes. Thus the inside of the body, in theory at least, became accessible to the knife. There was also at this time a massive growth of technical expertise in surgery. By 1840 surgeons were much more skilled than their predecessors, and, without anaesthesia, could skilfully reconstruct and remove damaged bones, joints and soft tissues. Again French surgeons had been world leaders in effecting this change, not least because the hospitals of Paris permitted ample scope for practice on the poor. By the 1840s, especially in France, surgeons were representing themselves as the great egalitarian heroes of modern life. Elite surgeons often prided themselves as ordinary folk made good. They were, they said, champions of scientific medicine applied to the miseries of the common people. If physic (the branch of medicine practised by the physician) was the élite medicine of an aristocratic world, surgery was the medicine of a democratic one. This does not mean to say surgeons were democratic reformers – many indeed were élite, establishment figures – rather, the model of disease they employed was that of the many, not the few. This is well illustrated by nineteenth-century American surgeons who pronounced surgery to be an art brought to perfection by what they considered quintessential American traits: individualism, democracy, inventiveness and heroism. In Britain, too, surgeons began to attain similar social prominence and likewise pronounced on the superiority of their branch of healing. Along with physicians the surgical élite taught and practised on the poor in the great hospitals and counted the noblest in the land among their clientele (Lawrence, C. 1992a). Given this 'rise of surgery' it is hardly surprising that the early nineteenth century saw numerous attempts to facilitate technical surgical practice, notably by rendering the patient unconscious. In the 1840s mesmeric techniques (which had radical political associations) and chemical agents were employed. The establishment finally settled on the politically safe ether, after a demonstration of its effects in Boston in 1846 (Winter 1991).[4] Chloroform was introduced shortly afterwards by the Scot, James Young Simpson. Contrary to the most common accounts which credit anaesthesia with a dramatic interventive role, the use of the technique did not produce any immediate transformation in surgery. Surgery had already been fairly dramatically transformed. By the late 1850s, however, anaesthesia was being paraded as the talisman of medical progress. It was a technology that demonstrated medicine's capacity to abolish pain. That was sufficient. Religious conservatives, who protested that, say, the pains of childbirth were to be understood theologically, were attempting to sustain an argument that was already losing credence in the face of a medicine that was redefining its role. Medicine, surgeons and physicians agreed, understood the laws of *life* and could intervene to re-establish their normal operations.

In other contexts, however, surgeons, physicians and hospital governors were forced to concede that all was not ideal. By the mid-nineteenth century, many of the small voluntary hospitals of the Enlightenment had been made into large centres of treatment for the poor. They had been joined too by Poor Law infirmaries. The wards of the largest of these hospitals, contemporaries agreed, were microcosms of the Victorian city. Periodically, especially in the surgical wards, epidemics of fever, gangrene, and wound sepsis would occur. Hospitalism, as this disaster was christened, seemed to be a new phenomenon. It evoked markedly varying responses, all of which have to be seen, ultimately, as political. One response was that of the sanitarians, notably Chadwick and Florence Nightingale. The sanitarian solution was to tear down these massive cathedrals of medicine and construct small hospitals in rural areas. Famously and significantly, John Simon and Florence Nightingale fell out over the projected rebuilding of St Thomas's Hospital in the early 1860s. Simon – surgeon, lecturer in pathology and government medical officer – wanted to rebuild the hospital in the centre of London (which it was eventually) and Nightingale wanted it moved to the suburbs. Nightingale's view of what a hospital should be was quite different from those who, as we shall see, were making them temples of interventive medicine (Rosenberg 1979). Statistics were employed on all sides in these debates, and to the sanitarians they demonstrated that rural hospitals were more salubrious than urban ones. But statistics were the instruments of argument, not the origin of the argument itself. Sanitarians saw the solutions to disorder in such things as legislation, engineering and architectural and moral reform. In one sense then, they did not see hospitalism as a medical issue at all. Indeed, their hostility was directed to what they perceived as the expansionist programme of medical men.

By contrast, surgeons (or at least some surgeons) perceived the solution to hospitalism to lie at the doctor–patient level, in a modification of surgical technique. This perception, like that of the sanitarians, was intricately embedded in a political agenda. A surgical solution to hospitalism could be used to maintain, indeed strengthen, the role of large teaching hospitals and the power of the medical profession both inside and outside of them. The abolition of hospitalism promised a valuable prize to whoever could convince the public it had been their doing. This was the context in which it is necessary to appraise the work of the most famous surgeon of the nineteenth century, Joseph Lister. Lister was a medical man who was prominent among the Victorian champions of naturalism (such as Darwin and Huxley). He was an eminent surgeon, practising in Glasgow, Edinburgh and finally London. He was a tireless propagandist for scientific education in medicine and a fervent advocate of the great hospital as the site of surgical therapy and the seat of medical teaching. He was at the forefront of the campaign for more recognition of the experimental sciences. In 1900 he was made a baron. He was regarded as a hero by the late Victorians and Edwardians in the way that explorers and engineers were (the cultural similarities are quite marked). But it is not simply our good fortune that we find in Lister a surgeon who happens to exemplify the attributes of what some Victorians regarded as the ideal medical man. Lister, with the help of his small circle, made himself into the embodiment of a number of cultural features on which a faction in Victorian society placed the highest value: naturalism, professionalism, gentility and heroism.

Lister's so-called 'antiseptic revolution' was in itself a trivial matter which many at the time considered to be little more than an interesting modification of surgical technique. Across the country (across Europe and America indeed) *all* surgeons were modifying their techniques. At the same time hospitals were being refurbished and installing new sanitary systems: the diet of patients got better, nursing care was radically changing, the quality of bandages improved considerably (Granshaw 1992). All these transformations permitted, by the end of the century, interventive surgery of a sort and on a scale impossible (but not unimaginable) fifty years earlier. Lister was to present this change in surgical mortality and morbidity as his achievement, based, as he declared, on scientific research into the hidden causes of wound sepsis. The problem of hospitalism, he declared, was simply a problem of properly treating wounds. Thus what the triumphant Listerians paraded as a scientific success in the 1890s was also a political victory (Lawrence and Dixey 1992). The sanitarians were vanquished and medical science, university medical education, large hospitals and above all naturalism were made into highly valued cultural products. Equally important, radical interventive treatment was transformed from an approach of last resort, carried out by a second class of healer, into a treatment of choice practised by new cultural heroes. We can see in this victory an occasion when dramatic therapeutic intervention was being honed into a powerful political tool (a point to which we shall return). We also see in it another example of the ways in which the medical profession, especially its party of science, were limiting the meanings of illness and recovery, by relating them to a medical capacity for technical intervention. Many Victorians celebrated that transformation by declaring the introduction of anaesthesia and antisepsis to be key moments in the history of progress.

The heroic story of the triumph of medical science later became one of the most visible features of the history of medicine in Victorian culture. It was a story soon shared by most medical men, and finally by the public. Those who would have told another story – the antivivisectionists, antivaccinationists, and many others – have left little trace. This triumphal history makes it hard to assess how far, at ground level, doctor–patient relations changed in the nineteenth century. According to contemporary accounts in the medical press, the profession was an autonomous body of practitioners. Its practice was governed by reference to science and personal experience, its internal hierarchy was organized in terms of skill and merit, and its judgements, whether at the bedside or in courts of law, were made only with regard to objective criteria (Crawford 1991). Such an ideology did important work in furthering medical interests. In different contexts, however, others admitted that things looked very unlike this.

For nearly all doctors everyday medical work meant private practice. Much as the profession might protest that its members were qualified by virtue of their education, many patients seemingly paid little heed to such things. At every level patients picked their doctors, either directly or by recommendation, by employing other criteria. Class background, education and manners figured large. Aristocratic patients sought out Oxbridge men who could hunt and shoot. In suburbia the middle classes chose doctors who were suitably devout and genteel (Peterson 1978). Practitioners who depended on working-class patients were very often contracted to so-called clubs and friendly societies and found themselves competing with others who offered their services for less. Some doctors flourished in this climate but many, both high and low, complained at the lack of appreciation of merit. As far as professional appointments were concerned, things were much the same. Selection for positions at voluntary hospitals depended on being well-connected either to the governors or the great physicians and surgeons and preferably to both. Being a gentleman counted for a great deal in making a successful medical career in the Victorian and Edwardian world.

Patronage in medicine continued, as in the eighteenth century, to have significance for the clinical encounter and prescribing habits. In many ways the clinical encounter at the end of the nineteenth century was quite different to that of the eighteenth century. From the late eighteenth century onwards doctors had been changing the concepts of disease with which they worked. Understanding sickness increasingly required skill in diagnosis, in discovering by clinical *examination* (notably physical examination) the specific tissue or organic disorder causing the symptoms. Expertise meant access to and use of a body of knowledge unfamiliar to the patient. The stethoscope, often depicted in the Victorian era, was emblematic of this modern approach to disease for both doctor and patient. By 1900 many other instruments, for example speculae, thermometers, pulse tracing devices, were also on hand, at least to the most self-consciously up-to-date practitioners (Reiser 1978). But if knowing and discovering were enshrined in the textbooks, and were turned into skills by medical students practising on the poor in the hospital, private medicine could be quite different. Whatever the best manuals said should be done, many doctors were reluctant to examine women or to use instruments. Explanations, examinations and prescriptions had to be tailored to patients' demands. In a telling quote which reveals both patient power and the place of the sick in hospital, Sir Clifford Allbutt, Regius Professor of Physic at Cambridge, recalled attempting to introduce a new diagnostic technique, 'I begged a lady of atonic fibre . . . to allow me to wash the stomach out. I begged in vain. Even hospital patients resented it at first' (Lawrence, C. 1985b). It is not surprising that patients dictated terms, they paid and doctors had no monopoly. There was after all, in the late nineteenth century, a flourishing army of unqualified healers, many of whom, although they did not compete on equal terms, were still regarded by some sections of the public as being no less competent than orthodox practitioners. Homeopathy was still immensely popular, and probably the most significant alternative (and often medicine of first choice) for many wealthy folk. For the poor and even the middle classes, local druggists (now calling themselves chemists) were always ready to give advice over the counter. Proprietary medicines were widely available and widely employed, especially preparations containing opium (Berridge and Edwards 1987).

Still, by the end of the nineteenth century we can legitimately talk of the medical profession, employing a term that would have been meaningful to contemporaries. The members of that profession began to call themselves doctors on the grounds that, as the *British Medical Journal* noted, the word 'conveys an implied compliment that we are, *par excellence*, the depositories of learning and the distributors of its fruits' (*BMJ* 1906, i: 757). Loosely we might describe that profession as middle class, but such a description hides as much as it reveals, for the profession contained all the finely nuanced class distinctions of the Edwardian world. At one end of the profession might be a general practitioner, perhaps the part-time employee of the Local Government Board. He (women were just about entering the profession in the 1880s) might have a lock-up surgery in the East End of London. Much of his time might be spent treating patients insured by working men's organizations – the clubs and friendly societies. Socially he was lower middle class, on a par with the schoolteacher, the modest clerk and the ordinary accountant. At the other end might be a man with a position on the staff of one of the large London voluntary hospitals with a teaching post at the attached medical school. He might sit on Royal Commissions and, perhaps, the General Medical Council. He might well have rooms in the West End, and, if a surgeon, employ beds at one of the many new private nursing homes springing up in the capital. His patients might be the aristocracy or wealthy city men and their families. Socially such doctors moved in quite different circles from their 'professional colleagues' in the East End. Sir Arthur Hurst remembered attending the surgical rounds at Guy's Hospital in 1901 when 'elaborate tie pins were still worn with morning dress. [Alfred, later Sir Alfred] Fripp always had his black tie adorned with a small diamond replica of the Prince of Wales's feathers, a favourite present of the Prince to his friends' (Hurst 1949, 43). By 1900 medical knighthoods littered the *Medical Directory*. It was often hard for women to make their way in this world. St Thomas's did not admit women students until 1947 (Lowndes 1956). Patients were expected to know their place. At St Bartholomew's Hospital, the physician, Sir Percival Horton-Smith-Hartley, when addressed by a patient as 'doctor' would reply '*Sir* my man. *Sir* my man' (Bourne 1963, 51). Writing in the *British Medical Journal* in 1932 the physician, Hugh Crichton-Miller advised any doctor embarking on private practice 'to acquaint himself with the main features of primitive man's psychology' (Crichton-Miller 1932).

In between the London 'great', as they were called, and those on the margins there was a spectrum of medical careers and nuanced social gradations. Provincial practice was no different. There could be a mighty economic, social and professional space between the practitioner in a mining village in Yorkshire, and a man with an appointment at one of the great northern hospitals. In cities like Sheffield, Manchester and Birmingham, private medical schools were loci which medical men transformed into red brick universities where appointment as professors fostered respectability and practice in the local community.

There was one attribute which regular medical men seem to have been more successful in developing than their competitors. Increasingly during the nineteenth century, practitioners, especially general practitioners, represented themselves as, and were increasingly taken to be, family doctors. In the eighteenth century, in situations where plenty of choice was available, a family might call on different practitioners for each member and indeed for each illness. In the Victorian age, if he was lucky, a doctor might be adopted by a family of paying patients and, unless specialist help were required, he might be the only practitioner ever called to the household (Loudon 1984). Many families warmly praised their doctor, valuing in particular his loyalty, dedication and friendship. In this context doctors began to develop the role of confidantes and moral advisors. In their medical schools young men were learning that medicine singularly equipped them to be students of the human condition. A knowledge of nature and clinical experience, they were taught, uniquely combined to give them insights unavailable to others. As W. H. Broadbent, a St Mary's Hospital physician, explained to the students in 1892,

The very business of our lives is the solution of intellectual problems of the most interesting character. On the large scale we see the working out of general laws. . . We note the vindication of the moral principles of right and wrong, the slow working of God's mill that grinds exceeding small.

(Lawrence, C. 1985b)

The sympathetic family doctor also began to flourish in the novel. Public endorsement of this advisorial role is a measure of the rising esteem of professionals as a whole. Many heads of families after all, were professional men themselves. It is also an indication of the increasing credibility given to scientific authority as a source of judgements, including moral ones. Of course, the trade was not all one way. The figure of the family doctor reinforced the Victorian valuation of the family.

By 1900, within this single profession of medicine, there were many occupations, many roles and many different languages were spoken. The voices of the less successful are more difficult to hear but, no doubt, their medical beliefs and healing practices were inflected with, for example, their methodism, socialism or spiritualism. Such allegiances might help to define where a medical man stood in the community and in relation to issues such as animal experimentation, compulsory vaccination, land reform, or the education of women.

But all medical voices were not equal and the predominant voice was that of the medical élite. Because medicine is so often regarded solely as a specialized occupation and perhaps, therefore, seen as relatively marginal to historical understanding of late Victorian and Edwardian society, the voice of élite medicine is often overlooked. Yet this medicine was a significant site in which the culture of late nineteenth-century Britain was created. It was medical men, and especially medical men of the élite, who provided many of the categories through which Victorians and Edwardians understood, explained, criticized and legitimated their world. At the most general level medical men had been significant promoters of scientific over religious authority. Medicine furnished both the agents, the doctors, and the rationalization, scientific naturalism, of this new authority. And it was the language of scientific naturalism which was increasingly used to explain and explore issues central to this society, such as urban criminality, the role of the family, the place of women, the division of labour, imperial expansion, racial difference and poverty (Smith, R. 1992).

To take one example, which touches all the foregoing features of turn of the century life; much of the language employed to explain the existence and behaviour of the dangerous classes in Victorian society was generated within the medical community (Mort 1987). By the late nineteenth century, doctors had produced a complex descriptive and explanatory language for understanding the origins and relations of, for example, race, criminality, madness, alcoholism, hereditary syphilis, imbecility and straightforward poverty. Theories of degeneration, in the main produced by medical men, linked these things together. Theories not only provided a global interpretation, they were resources which doctors could employ to make sense of professional encounters, the clinical consultation for instance. Such theories also justified management strategies, for example, institutionalization or eugenic intervention (Pick 1989). The latter was often promoted but rarely implemented in Britain (Jones 1986). The naturalistic seat of degeneration was the nervous system. This system, highly developed in the most intelligent and still evolving animal, man, was capable through natural (but morally initiated) causes, of degenerating (with loss of higher control) to display its more bestial or primitive racial elements. Mongolism, now called Down's syndrome, described in this context, was said to reveal this particularly well (Zihni 1989). Degeneration was a downward hereditary spiral in which mild moral deviance could lead, if unchecked, through the generations to the grossest animal manifestations. The nervous system in fact, was the crucial natural object through which the Victorians explained racial hierarchy, criminality, class difference and woman's 'femininity' and all that this entailed (Oppenheim 1991).

To say that medicine produced many of the cultural resources through which the Victorians understood their society is not to argue that medicine was, by itself, a fundamental *cause* of change, either cultural or social, in the nineteenth century. Medicine, as opposed to, say, religion, undoubtedly became much more important as a source of intellectual resources for understanding the world. But these resources were generated, used and endorsed in a wider context. Medical men had religious beliefs, they held political opinions, they had views about the role of women, the management of the poor, the condition of England question. Many doctors belonged to (and many more identified with) the affluent middle classes. Their attitudes and their naturalism were part of the culture of that class, not of an independent medical profession.

To talk of the medical élite is to speak of a group with some sense of identity but no detailed coherent programme. In, say 1890, there could have been a marked contrast in political and religious belief, and attitude to science, between a conservative consulting surgeon at St

Bartholomew's Hospital, London, and an agnostic, liberal professor of anatomy in a provincial medical school. Different sections of the medical élite guarded their own privileges and, for example, some clinical teachers viewed with concern the programmes of medical men promoting the basic sciences. Only later, as they gained authority over it, did clinicians fully embrace the laboratory (Jacyna 1988; Sturdy 1992b). Perceptions of what science was also varied among the élite, both over time and in different places, just as perceptions had varied between the élite minority and the reforming majority earlier in the century. Much of the new language of science and naturalism was the creation of the most self-consciously intellectual faction of the élite, especially the university teachers, notably those associated with University College London, Cambridge University and the Royal Society.

This group became much more prominent from the 1870s onwards, years which saw the beginnings of a shift in élite medicine towards a new form of scientific authority. Whereas earlier the élite had found its authority in the dissecting room, in the clinic or the statistical survey, at the end of the century it increasingly supplemented and supplanted these sources with the authority of the laboratory. Laboratory science, which to a great extent meant science based on animal experimentation, was, at first, principally a continental, and to a great extent a German, creation. Initially it was adopted and promoted in Britain by only a fraction of the medical élite and usually tied to the promotion of the role of the universities in medicine and the reform of medical education. Lister was a significant figure in this movement. Experimental physiology was an important cause for these reformers but, from the late 1880s onwards, the bacteriological laboratory became one of the most significant statements by medical men of their legitimate role in explaining and managing epidemic disease. The germ theory of specific infective diseases had been developed as a set of laboratory practices mainly in Germany in the 1870s and 1880s. It was quite unlike Lister's early germ theory which was much closer to the putrefactive theories abounding in the heyday of Victorian sanitary reform (Lawrence and Dixey 1992). Its adoption in the last two decades of the nineteenth century is significant for a number of reasons. The germ theory was, compared to previous new theories, relatively uncontested and formed an important site of consensus within medicine. Compared to the ideological warfare that characterized the theorizing about epidemic disease in the 1840s, this was remarkable. But conditions were quite different in the 1880s. For one, political opposition to the establishment from the rank-and-file had weakened and thus the deployment of alternative scientific theories had all but abated. The path to the acceptance of the new bacteriology had been eased by the relative success in the 1880s of what was now being known and acclaimed as 'Listerism'. This had vanquished opposition outside medicine (the sanitarians) and had also gone some way to establishing within it the centrality of animal experimentation and basic scientific research as the appropriate approach to the understanding of febrile disease.

The new germ theory proposed that biological agents, bacteria, were the cause of specific febrile diseases. It was thus a theory which, since it was biological, could be easily integrated into the other major naturalistic, biological theories of the day (evolution and cell theory). The biological agents which the new germ theory described as causing disease were, ultimately, defined by technological manipulations – culture, inoculation, plating out – in the laboratory. Once accepted, the theory entailed that the everyday understanding of disease causality was the prerogative of laboratory work (Cunningham 1992). In fact, by the 1890s, the laboratory's claim to define and establish the presence of febrile disease was relatively uncontested. Soon it was incontestable (Latour 1983). The laboratory's position as arbiter of the existence and nature of febrile disease was eventually extended to include most other conditions. Laboratory medicine was not of course autonomous. To a great extent it was used by the élite of hospital and university medicine to underwrite their authority (Jewson 1976). Because of the consensus that sustained germ theory, and because that consensus was not challenged outside medicine, the theory made the understanding and control of febrile disorder (in every sense) less of an overt political issue and more of a medical prerogative: an approach notably different from earlier sanitarian interventions. An outbreak of, say, typhus in the slums of Glasgow, was now a question to be addressed in a bacteriological laboratory. In this sense the laboratory was an instrument of gradual reform. Laboratory medicine could generate expert advice as to whether these or those local housing conditions had bred disease or whether this or that diet might be sufficient to nourish the poor. Such solutions were technical and not overtly political. They did not address the issue of whether an outbreak of typhus or malnourishment among certain groups in the population was fundamentally a political question about labour and the distribution of income.

At the bedside and in the realm of public health, germ theory was developed and employed in such a way as to reinforce a more general shift being effected as medicine became increasingly prominent in late nineteenth-century society. Listerism we have noted, 'solved' the problem of hospitalism by directing attention to the therapeutic encounter. This redirection was simply one instance of the many ways in which, as we also observed of John Simon's department, medical men as they became more influential in the politics of poverty, shifted concern from wholescale reform to personal intervention (by a doctor or other) at the individual level. Slowly but distinctly in the public health sphere, doctors moved their attention from environmental manipulation to the question of the individual's role in the production of disease; education about personal hygiene and diet (especially choice of diet) was perceived as crucial to the national health or lack of it. As one MOH wrote in 1896,

> Thousands, nay, hundreds of thousands, of young men and women with hereditary or acquired tendencies to various diseases are, owing to want of knowledge, brought up, enter upon occupations and lead modes of life which inevitably result in disease and early death.
>
> (Webb and Webb 1910)

The causes of tuberculosis were increasingly seen to lie in lack of personal cleanliness, irregular habits and moral laxity as well as bad housing (Worboys 1992a). Surveys which regularly revealed high morbidity and mortality rates among the poor were used by medical men as evidence for the necessity of intervention at the individual level. For example, the very high infant mortality of the Edwardian era was attacked primarily by the provision of health visitors, maternity services and infant welfare centres: that is by the direction of attention to individual mothers (Lewis 1992). The clinic, informed by the findings of the laboratory, was being installed as the solution to death and disease among the poor. This installation was effected by the redistribution and division of medical labour: pathologist, clinician, laboratory assistant, health visitor and many other workers inside and outside of hospitals were increasingly integrated into administrative hierarchies, often dominated by university departments (Sturdy 1992a).

This emphasis on individual responsibility reveals continuity with the eighteenth century, but there were also profound differences. In the eighteenth century, the illness which followed irresponsibility was, patient and doctor agreed, a deviation from the sufferer's own *natural* state. At any moment the disease was the whole condition of the sufferer, inseparable from him. In this context diagnosis, giving a sufferer's symptoms a name, was relatively easy and only a prelude to the more difficult task of elucidating the unique features of the case. By the end of the nineteenth century, diseases, even when regarded as engendered by self-neglect, were being designated specific, often isolable, biological processes, pathological deviations from the *normal* physiological processes of the population as a whole (Warner 1986).

Correspondingly, diagnosis was no longer a preliminary act, it was now the most significant and difficult clinical skill. Ideally, diagnosis was defined as going beyond the symptoms to the identification of the biological process that was common to all who suffered from the disease. In cases of fever such an ideal was becoming regular practice, and to diagnose, say typhoid, was to refer to a specific inflammatory process and this meant, in the end, a specific set of laboratory practices, a specific form of medical work.[5] For, in the bacteriology laboratory, disease processes were accounted reproducible in experimental animals, away from the ward and outside of the body of any particular sufferer.[6] Being specific processes and not idiosyncratic changes, it was argued, diseases were, or one day would be, amenable to specific therapeutic intervention (specific to the process that is, not to the sufferer). Laboratory medicine was indeed developed in just this direction: investigating the processes of and possible therapies for infectious and acute diseases.

In the three decades before the First World War a string of potent therapeutic and prophylactic agents appeared from the laboratory. These included Koch's tuberculin for tuberculosis, diphtheria antitoxin, salvarsan for syphilis and, during the first decade of the new century, a large number of gland extracts and therapeutic vaccines, although the claims made for many of these latter were eventually rejected as they were for tuberculin (Weindling 1992; Worboys 1992b; Chen 1992). The perceived potency of these agents was significant in promoting the view that the best medicine was technological intervention at the individual level to prevent or cure a specific disease process. More generally, endorsement of this view followed from the respect the Victorians and Edwardians increasingly accorded the sciences and the medical profession. In an era preoccupied with evolution, the claim that individual intervention had become scientific and effective was quickly coupled to the promise of social progress. The expectations of doctors began to be shared by reformers. We should not underestimate the confidence some Edwardians were beginning to have in the power of the clinic. For example, the Fabian socialists, Sidney and Beatrice Webb, when criticizing the inadequacy of Poor Law medical services, observed that tuberculosis, some forms of cancer, heart conditions, rheumatism and diabetes were all diseases which could be prevented by early medical intervention. Such intervention could lead to massive savings of money and the alleviation of personal suffering (Webb and Webb 1910). To this day clinical medicine has continued to claim credit for the decline in the incidence of diseases such as diphtheria and tuberculosis on the basis of its powers of intervention, when, as many critics pointed out, then and now, the incidence fell as the housing and diet of the population improved (McKeown 1979; Weindling 1992).

As important as the growing view that individual intervention was the key to better national health was the democratization associated with this change. From socialist and New Liberal perspectives it was increasingly regarded as a mark of progress (civilization) that somehow either the state or charity or both should make provision for treatment to be available to all. From there it was not much of a step for some to regard such therapy as the right of each individual. This was a position that establishment physicians, not surprisingly, were ready to endorse. In 1918, Bertrand Dawson, author of the Dawson report, later the king's physician, wrote, 'the best means for procuring health and curing disease should be available for every citizen by right and not by favour' (Dawson 1918).

We can see that, by the beginning of the twentieth century, an account of the role of medicine in an industrial society had been created even if it was not explicitly formulated by any one author. This role was intricately related to new perceptions of health. Health, as Dawson's remark indicates, was beginning to be regarded as a right. But the idea of health as a right was being tied tightly to medicine's claimed ability, based on science, to intervene effectively in actual disease processes or preventatively in potential disease processes. As health was increasingly tied to the putative power of clinical intervention, so such intervention was beginning to be regarded as a means to deal with the problems of poverty. Medical intervention was seen as a powerful instrument for effecting the social progress and increasing national prosperity which some were convinced must occur. The first two decades of the new century saw this view of medicine increasingly appear on the conventional political stage.

Not surprisingly during these years the clinical consultation appeared prominent in the profession's account of its work. As the identification of disease processes and intervention in them was made into a function of expertise, so the doctor's opinion was made relatively more unquestionable. The language of privacy, sacredness and inviolable clinical judgement permeates the medical literature of the period. The ethics and etiquette of relations between patient and doctor were sources of great concern.[7] Consulting, of course, had always been central to medical practice. But doctors talked very little about the practical ethics of such situations and often felt little need to do such things as protect the names of their patients. In the late Victorian and Edwardian period doctors began to elaborate on the uniqueness of the clinical encounter and emphasize their role within it when, as we have seen, in the eighteenth century the patient had a significant active part. This concern with professional judgement was, in some respects, simply a response to the much resented and increasing control of the doctor's work by Poor Law Guardians or friendly societies (Honigsbaum 1979). It was more than this, however. It made medical work accountable only to other doctors – only to those with experience of the clinical situation. Here lay the origins of a language which privileged clinical judgement over any other consideration, such as the overtly political or the economic. This change can be perceived in other areas which doctors regarded as part of their province, such as abortion. During the nineteenth century, doctors pressed for abortion law reform, notably for any abortion not carried out by the profession, at any time in pregnancy, to be ruled illegal. Reform took this route. By the end of the nineteenth century a legal abortion could only be carried out by a doctor on what were deemed 'therapeutic' grounds, that is based solely on a clinical judgement about maternal health (Keown 1988). In the late nineteenth and early twentieth century, political and medical perspectives mutually reinforced each other. In a period during which it was increasingly accepted that in some degree the state should take responsibility for the health and welfare of its citizens, the very notion of what sort of intervention best promoted health and welfare was slowly being redefined. Although medical intervention had many meanings, prophylactic and therapeutic intervention at the individual level, initiated by privately practising doctors, were beginning to be accounted things of the highest value. This change can be detected in medicine's visual presentation of itself. Slowly, individual hospital patients, not wards or waiting rooms (spaces of charitable care), were made prominent in pictures of medical life (Fox and Lawrence 1988).

By 1900, from some perspectives, the medical profession in Britain already had a bounded character. Medical men of all sorts frequently alluded to professional goals, professional ethics, codes of conduct and so forth. They talked, in some contexts, as though they were united and, in some ways, they were. They had an organization, the British Medical Association (BMA), to represent their interests. Ideological conflict of the sort that rocked the 1840s had disappeared. General practitioners no longer generated alternative sciences, and medical education, emanating from the top, met with relative compliance from those below. The political dimensions of medical knowledge were largely absent or invisible. The public too, in many contexts, perceived the doctors as constituting a single profession. *Punch* cartoonists produced stereotyped pictures of medical men wearing top hats and carrying stethoscopes. Manufacturers and retailers advertised suits and motor cars, made specially for the medical man. Those who still drove carriages in London prided themselves that a doctor's horse could not be commandeered to draw a fire engine in an emergency (Taylor 1970). In some situations, therefore, professional society apparently hung together. Yet in many others it was severely fractured. By 1911 nearly half of the general practitioners in Britain were engaged in some form of contract practice (Honigsbaum 1979, 13). In many instances doctors were absolutely dependent on these contracts and most thought friendly society interference excessive and the remuneration far too inadequate for their professional expertise. A still overpopulated profession, however, was not in a strong position to bargain. The general practitioners complained not only about the friendly societies. The hospital practitioners, now being called consultants, were also a source of grief. Consultants exploited the club system, limiting the general practitioner's skills in favour of their own specialist expertise (Honigsbaum 1979). The BMA had been formed in the mid-nineteenth century as an instrument of agitation by the general practitioners. By 1900 it, and the GMC, were regarded by many of the rank-and-file as agencies, indeed class agencies, used by 'medical aristocrats' (the consultants) to crush the general practitioners and their claims for more reward (Larking 1907). Some general practitioners strove to convert the BMA into a trade union with the right to strike (Marsh 1908). Around 1900, of course, many trade unions, especially craft unions, were élite groupings which excluded unskilled labour. Poorer doctors obviously had no difficulty identifying with such organizations. Thus although from some perspectives we can see, as did contemporaries, medical men comprising a new professional class, we can also see medicine as occupationally divided and differentiated by many of the class distinctions that characterized Edwardian Britain.

Lloyd George's National Health Insurance (NHI) Act of 1911 was, eventually, to be one of the means by which the conflict between hospital consultant and general practitioner was scaled down, although by no means dissolved. This scaling down followed from the ways in which the Act was used to consolidate the ideological and political importance of private practice and individual intervention. These unifying effects followed from the interpretation and extension of the Act's provisions for medical attention for sick workers.

By the end of the nineteenth century there was, roughly speaking, a threefold division of orthodox medicine in Britain. First there was the private sector. This comprised a number of routes for delivering medical attention to the individual who, either directly or indirectly, paid a privately contracting practitioner. Included in this sector was the club or friendly society system, since, although practitioners were contracted to clubs, these were arrangements outside of the government sphere. The ultimate focus of the private sector was the doctor–patient consultation for sickness (and childbirth). The most important and most public face of the private sector was the great voluntary hospital. Here the élite of private practitioners practised publicly and charitably. Because of an admissions policy that inclined such hospitals to favour acute cases, but also because the élite was increasingly defining excellence in medicine as scientifically-derived clinical intervention, the medicine practised at the voluntary institutions began to be perceived by some as unrepresentative. The hospital consultants were criticized for taking too much interest in 'the acute case and the unique or "interesting" case' (Webb and Webb 1910, 152). Much of the second sector of medicine – under the Poor Law – was oriented to the same end as the private sector, clinical contact, but its character was quite different. Under the Poor Law, doctors were employed as District Medical Officers. They also attended the sick in work houses. In Poor Law infirmaries doctors could gain full or part-time positions. These men were ultimately regulated by the Local Government Board (the LGB, a central government department) and they were effectively state employees. By 1911 there was plenty of work for these doctors. Poor Law hospitals, for example, contained twice as many beds as voluntary institutions (Lewis 1992, 321). Much Poor Law work involved visiting patients living in wretched conditions and dispensing (often criticized as peremptory) for chronic complaints such as longstanding tuberculosis, varicose ulcers or bedsores. The third medical sector was the domain of public health. It was here that the MOH worked either part or full time, in the employ of a local authority. By 1910 extensive therapeutic services (including hospitals) were also provided by municipalities. Much medical work in this domain, therefore, was also individual, examining school children for example (Frazer 1950, 256). It is noteworthy that the public health doctors were as differentiated by class, qualification, attitudes to trade unionism and prestige of their appointments, as the private practitioners were (Porter, D. 1991).

The NHI Act of 1911 was the outcome of a number of general and local forces. At the most general level it derived from new political concerns, notably those addressed in New Liberal and socialist circles. Here interest centred on formulating long term social policy about such things as wages, unemployment, education and welfare (Freeden 1978). In part this stemmed from worries about national efficiency – concern with the physical state of the poor. This state had been starkly revealed in the examination of recruits for the Boer War. The feeble condition of many of the men led some to wonder whether the Empire itself might be in danger. Lloyd George famously remarked that a C_3 population would not do for an A_1 empire (Lewis 1992, 326). Between 1906 and 1914 the Liberal Party addressed these issues in a number of welfare measures, for instance, old age pensions and unemployment insurance. The organization and financing of medical care at this time was very much subordinate to wider concerns.

Lloyd George's Act of 1911, in line with other broad approaches to welfare, was initially framed to protect the wages of sick workers. Lloyd George, like Chadwick, regarded sickness as an important cause of poverty. From left and right, such straightforward approaches to relief were attacked for failing to encourage the poor to be thrifty or improve themselves. Lloyd George modified his proposals. The allowance would provide income maintenance for the sick and access to medical care, the latter conditional on the patient's good character (Fox 1986a).

Although there was hostility to Lloyd George's plans in the higher ranks of the BMA, most doctors were willing to assist in the provision of medical care on various conditions, notably that there was no suggestion of any form of state service or at least any form that intruded into private practice. In its first formulation the Act appeared to the doctors to be an extension of the contract system, and Christopher Addison, a member of the BMA's advisory committee, observed that it 'simply stank in the nostrils of the whole medical profession' (Morgan and Morgan 1980, 13). It is not hard to see why. The great physicians feared even the slightest hint of involvement with state service. After all many of them gave their services charitably, one of the distinctions of a gentleman. Private practice could be extraordinarily lucrative. At the top, it furnished a comfortable and genteel lifestyle. There was concern among the more humble practitioners that state service would result in relative impoverishment. Relations with Poor Law Guardians and friendly societies had already produced a distaste for salaried employment. None the less, this distaste had other roots. Gentility was as much a desired status among the lowly practitioners as with the mighty and, relatedly, the right to choose – to contract independently – was a deeply cherished medical ideology. Other forces were at work too. By the time of the Act, trade unionism in general had become more militant and had been extended more widely among manual labourers (Thomson 1984). Except in relatively small numbers, the doctors never flirted with socialism. As unionism increasingly became identified with socialism and with manual labour, general practitioners no longer perceived unionization as desirable. Intraprofessional conflict ceased to look like a class war as the majority, effectively, moved to the right. It was the medical profession's individualism, conservativism, commitment to gentility, and the significance it (and increasingly others) accorded to intervention in disease processes that had important influence on the form and consequences of the 1911 Act.

The NHI Act of 1911 was an intervention into welfare provision at the level of the private sector. Some, such as the Webbs, who were agitating for welfare and health reform campaigned for intervention at the level of the Poor Law or in the public health sphere (Webb and Webb 1910); the point being that alternative interventions into health care were open to the government. Lloyd George's Act, by way of insurance, provided sickness benefits and access to a doctor – a private clinician – for workers. Reform in other words signalled state involvement in the provision of private treatment for sickness. To organize the health insurance programme Lloyd George chose a minister, Charles Masterman, and a civil servant, Robert Morant, both of whom were enthusiastic believers in medical services as means to promote social progress. Reform was eventually welcomed by the doctors since it freed them from the control of the hated friendly societies. Doctors – general practitioners – were much better off under the new system and were no longer subject to the decisions of a club committee. Doctors could build up a 'panel' of patients to any size they desired. During the inter-war years, general practitioners' incomes rose relatively and absolutely (Digby and Bosanquet 1988).[8] The NHI Act was a triumph for voluntarism, the clinical encounter and, less obviously but equally real, gentility.

The potential in the Act for developing a central role for clinical medicine was quickly exploited. By the end of the First World War what had begun as a policy to avoid destitution was transmuted into a policy of access to medical consultation. Perceptions of medical success during the war, notably in surgery, helped bring this about. An example of this transformation can be seen in the government's establishment of VD clinics. The issue of VD was central to debates about welfare, racial health, national efficiency and morals. When a Royal Commission was set up to report on VD in 1913, the *Lancet* envisaged that the enquiry would examine the issue solely from diagnostic and therapeutic perspectives. Feminists and social purity groups lobbied to have such issues as prostitution and overcrowding investigated. The social origins of VD, however, were by-passed. The 'scourge' of VD was 'solved' by the creation of clinics, where the microscope, drugs and individual moral instruction addressed the problem (Evans 1992). The growing weight accorded to medical intervention was capitalized on in the creation of a Ministry of Health in the summer of 1919. All the key posts went to figures associated with NHI and all the sections of the LGB fell under its auspice. Addison was the first minister. The LGB's chief medical officer, Arthur Newsholme, a promoter of salaried schemes, was forced to retire. The Ministry of Health was not a ministry of health at all, it was a ministry of clinical medicine.[9] Its first major activities were solving problems about the extension of medical care, such as providing specialist treatment and hospital facilities. Since 1920 the primary debate about social welfare has been how to organize and deliver clinical medical services to the population as a whole (Fox 1986a). The NHS of 1948 was another solution to that problem (Webster 1988).

Many of these trends in the 1920s were summed up, and approved, by Sir George Newman who had displaced Arthur Newsholme when the Ministry of Health was created. Newman gave an account of the medical past and future in his little book of 1931, *Health and Social Evolution*. In this work Newman explained how medicine and social progress were inseparable. He observed that universal education, an improved environment, cooperation, and a 'new moral order' were principles of 'modern collective humanism'. These principles, he noted, were 'expressed through the science and art of medicine'. Fundamental to the expression of the principles, he observed, was that doctors and the state were 'working to secure the same ends'. In this regard he noticed how a salaried medical service was incompatible with true democracy. Cooperation between the state and the doctor, he said, was founded on the fact 'that the doctor was an *individualist* . . . practising as a scientific man'. Only under the circumstances where the practitioner was free to choose could the medical or surgical advice given by the doctor be 'the best exercise of his skill'. Turning to the history of public health he referred to 'The old idea of Preventive Medicine being exclusively concerned with "drains and stinks", or with quarantine and the isolation of patients suffering from infectious diseases, or even the later view that its particular sphere was the external environment'. These approaches, he said, belonged to the past. Today, he ruled, the torch of preventative medicine has passed on to 'the epidemiologist, the pathologist, the immunologist, the anaesthetist, the bacteriologist, the antiseptic surgeon, and the general medical practitioner'. All of these, it should be noted, with the possible exception of the epidemiologist, were clinical workers, laboratory scientists or a combination of both. Newman was right: in many ways clinical medicine and public policy on health were becoming one. The clinical encounter was medicine's most significant moment: clinically, diseases were being described in ways which emphasized the individual's responsibility, but the causal processes were accounted for in ways that privileged only the intervention of the medical expert. The redescription of heart disease in the 1920s is a particularly good example of this (Bartley 1985; Lawrence, C. 1992b). Explaining the individual's role, Newman noted that medicine had through 'biology, physiology and aetiology' learned the laws of nature. But it was now the task of Everyman to be 'obedient to her laws', for the torch of public health progress had now passed to Everyman. 'For the maintenance of health and capacity, physical and mental, is now the quest of Everyman, and until it is the daily habit of Everyman we shall not as a people possess this particular treasure' (Newman 1931, 126–70).

Conclusion and the beginning

By the time of the creation of the Ministry of Health many of the principal features – professional, organizational, institutional, cognitive – of twentieth-century British medicine had been created. By 1920 a single profession, but not occupation, of medicine existed. It was relatively bounded, with a high degree of control over its work and over that of other fields such as nursing or midwifery. Effectively most medical practitioners were private practitioners and more were to become so as the Poor Law was dismantled. The profession as a whole had achieved a fair degree of influence and was the first and sometimes the only body to be consulted by government in matters of health. Politically, by the 1920s, there was a commitment to the provision of medical services for the whole population, and this, to a great extent, meant individual therapeutic and preventative services. There was too, by this time, some measure of agreement among politicians of all main parties, analysts and doctors that the most efficient way to deliver these services was through hierarchies of institutions and practitioners, regionally organized. The consensus that proper organization of clinical services was the key to health hardened during the inter-war years. Disagreement centred on how this organization could best be achieved; how to integrate the various sorts of hospital service for example. Seen in this light the NHS was the not very radical outcome of negotiation and mutual accommodation among various interested groups (Fox 1986b).

Already by 1920 the hospitals were at the top of the regional hierarchies. The middle classes were now entering hospitals as paying patients. Even royalty would eventually consent to hospital admission. During the 1930s, innovation in the organization of medical care was focused primarily on hospitals. They were increasingly graded by the sophistication of their staff and their technology. In medical practice hierarchy meant occupational division: the most obvious distinction being between the hospital consultants and the GPs. In hospitals 'firms' of junior and senior staff were created fulfilling educational aims and the ideal of coordinated, hierarchical teamwork (Cooter 1993). The hospital surgeons were a particularly powerful group. Many GPs were esteemed, trusted and valued as sources of clinical and moral advice. Since the 1920s, public health medicine has been, relatively, on the wane. Local authority work with its hint of socialism and state service was never popular with the private medical sector. Indeed as a result of recent reforms the MOH has disappeared altogether. To some extent the responsibilities of former public health officials have been transferred to the realm of curative medicine.[1]

One notable and related feature of medical expansion since the 1920s has been the increasing prominence of science and laboratory research. Nevertheless, even then the conviction that laboratory science was the route to health was widely shared. The diagnostic or clinical laboratory was perceived as the cornerstone of sound practice and the research laboratory was seen as the site where scientific investigation would generate the knowledge through which disease would be conquered. Indeed, state provision for laboratory facilities for research can be traced to the 1911 Act, in which a small amount of money was made available to fund medical work on tuberculosis. This provision was interpreted and expanded to effect the creation of what eventually became the Medical Research Council (MRC), the government grant-giving body funding scientific research, much of it laboratory based (Austoker and Bryder 1989).

Culturally, the place of medicine in British life looked not so very different in 1920 from the way it appears now. Medicine was perceived as an important agent, perhaps the most important, for ameliorating the human lot. But it was a particular sort of medicine. Medicine was the encounter between doctor and acutely ill – especially the acutely-ill young. In this encounter powerful technologies – electrical and X-ray machinery figured significantly in the 1920s – were prominent. The disease model used by doctors stressed the role of individual responsibility in the production of pathology. But, unlike earlier models, in this account the pathology was not peculiar to the individual. Diseases were regarded as specific processes, defined by laboratory work. Increasingly, the profession designated the best medical practice as therapeutic or preventative intervention in these processes. By 1920 such intervention was beginning to be perceived as every citizen's right, and a necessary good. This view became commonplace later in the century. That any and every sickness, in any and every person should be, and must be, addressed in this way became, for a while, almost incontestable. What is striking about this view of medicine is that it crossed all party-political lines. It appeared apolitical and obvious. That, in this perception, there was a perfect conjunction of moral right, technical means and the general good can be measured by the well-known fact that, at the inception of the NHS, it was widely anticipated that medical costs would gradually fall as the service delivered health to the nation.

That the proper terms for discussing the health of the population are the number of doctors per thousand population or the number of hospital beds still seems reflexively true for most politicians, at least in public pronouncements. Many people, however, have begun to ask whether the predominance of a certain sort of acute medicine has prohibited serious discussion of, for example, provision of *care* for the mad, the chronically sick, the elderly, the poor, the disabled; and whether the public's health has suffered at the expense of the clinic; and whether understanding and coming to terms with suffering is as important as intervening. Since the 1970s some have begun to wonder whether the interventive clinical medicine that we have is the appropriate or only cultural form for delivering national *health*. One of the aims of this book is to help situate current criticisms of medicine, to show where they are part of the twentieth-century organizational and professional tradition and where, often unwittingly, they question ideas, assumptions and practices which were fabricated deep in the historical strata but which are still very much with us.

Notes

INTRODUCTION

1 But see Doyal and Pennel 1979, which concentrates more on public health and is valuable for its account of other ways in which medicine could have been shaped. For a similar story about the United States see Rosenberg 1987.
2 I say 'so-called', not pejoratively, but because it is hard to see how holistic understanding can be found in any system which is built on the cognitive foundations of orthodox medicine.
3 This seems to have been less the case for the earlier period covered here.

1 THE ENLIGHTENMENT

1 In other words, with extremely rare exceptions, there was no role for doctors as, for example, inspectors or advisors on affairs of state. Not all medical practice involved personal contact. Consultation by letter was common in the eighteenth century.
2 Specific causality is central to modern medicine. Designating a specific cause at some level, for instance, endocrinological (e.g. thyroid deficiency), morbid anatomical (e.g. coronary thrombosis), bacteriological (e.g. streptococcal tonsillitis) or chemical (e.g. asbestosis), defines the disease. Several levels of specific causation can also be designated e.g. hypercholesterolaemia causing atherosclerosis and, in turn, coronary thrombosis.
3 The wealthy were quite aware that many medical men pretended to this level of accomplishment by buying their degrees; famously at St Andrews University in Scotland.
4 Hidden or inaccessible to the senses does not mean that orthodox medicine did not have visual knowledge of the inside of the body. University medical courses included anatomy teaching, and anatomical accounts of the abdominal, thoracic and cranial contents were very sophisticated. But the causes of disease were not often conceptualized as a particular, permanent changes in the anatomy of an area or a single organ. Rather they were dynamic, changing relations between fluids and solids and, in that sense, could not be visualized or touched.
5 Such advice manuals have a long history. It is the profusion of them that characterizes the eighteenth century.

6 Plague epidemics are a notable instance, before the eighteenth century, when great stress was laid on dirt and where, in some societies, general measures were effected by mobilizing medical men (Cipolla 1992).

2 THE AGE OF REFORM

1 Soul and mind were used synonymously in many contexts.
2 In many ways phrenology has the characteristics of a natural history of the cerebral surface. However, it was produced within a context in which the deep structure of the nervous system was being reformulated (Clarke and Jacyna 1987).
3 Although the physician's skill lay in reasoning to hidden causes, such causes were not defined by anatomical organization (or disorganization) identifiable by the senses.
4 In fact, French medicine had two classes of official practitioner: fully trained medical men and more menial practitioners who worked largely in country areas, the officiers de santé (Heller 1978).
5 Cooper had formed radical connections when young and in Edinburgh.
6 This did not mean living things were simply machines whose actions could be explained by the laws of physics. The animate world was deemed to have laws peculiar to itself but, said Lawrence and others, no reference need be made to superadded immaterial principles to explain these laws. Making the body into an object to be studied by a special science of life was, of course, making it a special object of medical study.
7 Bentham had drafted an Anatomy Act in 1826.
8 Out relief or out-door relief, was assistance given to the poor who were not in a workhouse.
9 Statistics had much more the meaning of fact gathering and classification, rather than complex mathematical analysis. Classified facts were held to reveal laws (Eyler 1979). Chadwick was very selective in the facts he gathered.
10 For example the concept of normal (with the sense of ideal, right or proper) body weight (adjusted for height, etc.) comes from this approach. The wider ramifications of normality are apparent if we consider the broader cultural meanings of obesity and slimness.
11 Sanitary reformers came from a broad political spectrum, and were by no means all utilitarians.
12 Chadwick himself seems not to have adopted Malthus's fatalism and relied more on the optimistic 'natural laws' described by political economists such as Ricardo (Finer 1952).

3 MODERNITY

1 It was, of course, various parties within government who valued medical intervention.
2 The importance of more regular bureaucratic forms should not be overlooked. In 1872, Simon's department was incorporated into a new Local Government Board. This was in many ways the continuation of the central authority which oversaw the administration of the Poor Law.

3 Vaccination and inoculation are interventions into potential disease processes.
4 That is, ether was chosen because it was not associated with radical philosophies.
5 I say ideally, because, as contemporaries recognized, many diseases, for example diabetes, were still identified by symptoms or classified by a variety of pathological criteria.
6 Whether or not animals suffer is not the point here: what counts is the reproduction of pathological features. In the twentieth century, disease processes are accounted reproducible *outside* of *any* living body. Tissue culture has been the relevant technology.
7 Privacy was very much a function of gender and class (McLaren 1993).
8 Interpretations of the Act discriminated between panel and individual private patients. In 1924 the Ministry of Health and the BMA agreed that in instances in which panel patients would make one half of the total net income of a doctor, only two-sevenths of the practitioners' time was to be assumed to be devoted to such work (Digby and Bosanquet 1988, 82).
9 The point is that the clinic was seen as the best way to deliver health, not that the Ministry was only concerned with acute care. There was still some sympathy in the Ministry for salaried service and Addison had long voiced concern that too much attention was given to curative over preventative medicine (Honigsbaum 1993, Addison 1914). One of the most famous proposals for reorganizing health care in these years, the Dawson report of 1920, often seen as a blueprint for the NHS, was an attempt to promote private practice against what was perceived as creeping statism (Webster 1993).

CONCLUSION AND THE BEGINNING

1 Reflecting on why this occurred a former MOH observed, 'ordinary doctors who treat sick people are trained to screw up the loose nuts and bolts when people are ill; they have no knowledge of public health work . . . but the government turned to them for advice' (Eastwood 1992, 49).

Bibliography

Abel-Smith, B. (1964) *The Hospitals, 1800–1948: A Study in Social Administration in England and Wales*, London: Heinemann.

Ackerknecht, Erwin H. (1948) 'Anticontagionism between 1821 and 1867', *Bulletin of the History of Medicine*, XX, 562–93.

Ackerknecht, Erwin H. (1967) *Medicine at the Paris Hospital*, Baltimore: Johns Hopkins University Press.

Addison, Christopher (1914) 'Medical Men: Their Place and Influence in the State', *British Medical Journal*, i, 379–82.

Andrew, Donna (1989) *Philanthropy and Police: London Charity in the Eighteenth-Century*, Princeton: Princeton University Press.

Austoker, Joan and Linda Bryder (eds) (1989) *Historical Perspectives on the Role of the MRC: Essays in the History of the Medical Research Council of the United Kingdom and its Predecessor, the Medical Research Committee, 1913–1953*, Oxford: Oxford University Press.

Barker-Benfield, J. (1992) *The Culture of Sensibility: Sex and Society in Eighteenth-Century Britain*, Chicago: The University of Chicago Press.

Bartley, Mel (1985) 'Coronary Artery Disease and the Public Health', *Sociology of Health and Illness*, VII, 289–313.

Berman, Morris (1978) *Social Change and Scientific Organization: The Royal Institution, 1799–1844*, London: Heinemann Educational Books.

Berridge, V. and Edwards, G. (1987) *Opium and the People*, London: Allen Lane.

Bourne, Geoffrey (1963) *We Met at Bart's: The Autobiography of a Physician*, London: Frederick Muller Ltd.

Brewer, John (1988) *The Sinews of Power: War, Money and the English State 1688–1783*, London: Hutchinson.

Bynum, W.F. (1981) 'Cullen and the Study of Fevers in Britain 1760–1820', in W.F. Bynum and V. Nutton (eds) *Theories of Fever from Antiquity to the Enlightenment*, *Medical History*, Supplement 1, London: Wellcome Institute for the History of Medicine, 135–48.

Chadwick, Edwin (1965) *Report on the Sanitary Condition of the Labouring Population of Great Britain (1842)*, edited with an Introduction by M.W. Flinn, Edinburgh: Edinburgh University Press.

Chen, Wai (1992) 'The Laboratory as Business: Sir Almroth Wright's Vaccine Programme and the Construction of Penicillin', in Andrew Cunningham and Perry Williams (eds) *The Laboratory Revolution in Medicine*, Cambridge: Cambridge University Press, 295–303.

Cipolla, Carlo M. (1992) *Miasmas and Disease: Public Health and the Environment in the Pre-Industrial Age*, New Haven and London: Yale University Press.

Clarke, Edwin and L.S. Jacyna (1987) *Nineteenth-Century Origins of Neuroscientific Concepts*, Berkeley, CA: University of California Press.

Cooter, R. (1982) 'Anticontagionism and History's Medical Record', in P. Wright and A. Treacher (eds) *The Problem of Medical Knowledge*, Edinburgh: Edinburgh University Press, 87–108.

Cooter, R. (1984) *The Cultural Meaning of Popular Science: Phrenology and the Organization of Consent in Nineteenth-Century Britain*, Cambridge: Cambridge University Press.

Cooter, R. (ed.) (1988) *Studies in the History of Alternative Medicine*, Basingstoke: Macmillan.

Cooter, R. (1991) 'Dichotomy and Denial: Mesmerism, Medicine and Harriet Martineau', in Marina Benjamin (ed.) *Science and Sensibility: Gender and Scientific Enquiry, 1780–1945*, Oxford: Basil Blackwell, 144–73.

Cooter, R. (1993) *Surgery and Society in Peace and War: Orthopaedics and the Organization of Modern Medicine*, Basingstoke: Macmillan.

Crawford, Catherine (1991) 'A Scientific Profession: Medical Reform and Forensic Medicine in British Periodicals of the Early Nineteenth Century', in Roger French and Andrew Wear (eds) *British Medicine in an Age of Reform*, London: Routledge, 203–30.

Crichton-Miller, H. (1932) 'Primitive Man and the Modern Patient', *British Medical Journal*, ii, 430–2.

Cunningham, Andrew (1992) 'Transforming Plague: The Laboratory and the Identity of Infectious Disease', in Andrew Cunningham and Perry Williams (eds) *The Laboratory Revolution in Medicine*, Cambridge: Cambridge University Press, 209–44.

Dawson, Bertrand (1918) 'The Future of the Medical Profession', *Lancet*, ii, 83–5.

Desmond, Adrian (1989) *The Politics of Evolution, Morphology, Medicine and Reform in Radical London*, Chicago: The University of Chicago Press.

Digby, Anne and Nick Bosanquet (1988) 'Doctors and Patients in an Era of National Health Insurance and Private Practice, 1913–1938', *The Economic History Review*, XLI, 74–94.

Donnison, J. (1977) *Midwives and Medical Men: A History of Interprofessional Rivalries and Women's Rights*, London: Heinemann Educational Books.

Douglas, M. (1966) *Purity and Danger*, London: Routledge & Kegan Paul.

Doyal, Lesley and Imogen Pennel (1979) *The Political Economy of Health*, London: Pluto Press.

Dupree, Marguerite W. and M. Anne Crowther (1991) 'A Profile of the Medical Profession in Scotland in the Early Twentieth Century: The Medical Directory as a Historical Source', Bulletin of the History of Medicine, LXV, 209–33.

Durey, M. (1979) *The Return of the Plague: British Society and the Cholera 1831–2*, Dublin: Gill & Macmillan.

Eastwood, Cyril G. (1992) *The Life and Death of The Medical Officer of Health*, Braunton, Devon: Merlin Books.

Elston, M.A. (1987) 'Women and Anti-Vivisection in Victorian England', in N.A. Rupke (ed.) *Vivisection in Historical Perspective*, London: Croom Helm, 259–94.

Evans, David (1992) 'Tackling the "Hideous Scourge": The Creation of the Venereal Disease Treatment Centres in Early Twentieth-Century Britain', *Social History of Medicine*, V, 413–34.

Eyler, J.M. (1979) *Victorian Social Medicine: The Ideas and Methods of William Farr*, Baltimore: Johns Hopkins University Press.

Figlio, Karl M. (1976) 'The Metaphor of Organisation: A Historiographical Perspective on the Bio-Medical Sciences of the Early Nineteenth Century', *History of Science*, XIV, 17–53.

Finer, S.E. (1952) *The Life and Times of Sir Edwin Chadwick*, London: Methuen.

Fissell, Mary E. (1991) *The Physic of Charity: Health and Welfare in the West Country, 1690–1810*, Cambridge: Cambridge University Press.

Foucault, M. (1970) *The Order of Things: An Archaeology of the Human Sciences*, London: Tavistock.

Foucault, M. (1973) *The Birth of the Clinic*, London: Tavistock.

Foucault, M. (1979) *Discipline and Punish: The Birth of the Prison*, Harmondsworth: Penguin Books.

Fox, Daniel M. (1986a) *Health Policies Health Politics: The British and American Experience 1911–1965*, Princeton: Princeton University Press.

Fox, Daniel M. (1986b) 'The National Health Service and the Second World War: The Elaboration of Consensus', in Harold L. Smith (ed.), *War and Social Change: British Society in the Second World War*, Manchester: Manchester University Press, 32–57.

Fox, Daniel M. and Christopher Lawrence (1988) Photographing Medicine: Images and Power in Britain and America since 1840, London: Greenwood Press.

Frazer, W.M. (1950) *A History of English Public Health, 1834–1939*, London: Baillière, Tindall & Cox.

Freeden, Michael (1978) *The New Liberalism: An Ideology of Social Reform*, Oxford: Clarendon Press.

French, R.D. (1975) *Antivivisection and Medical Science in Victorian Society*, Princeton: Princeton University Press.

French, Roger and Andrew Wear (eds) 1991 *British Medicine in an Age of Reform*, London: Routledge.

Geison, Gerald (1978) *Michael Foster and the Cambridge School of Physiology: The Scientific Enterprise in Late Victorian Society*, Princeton: Princeton University Press.

Gelfand, Toby (1972) 'The "Paris Manner" of Dissection: Student Anatomical Dissection in Early Eighteenth-Century Paris', *Bulletin of the History of Medicine*, XLVI, 99–130.

Ginzburg, Carlo (1980) 'Morelli, Freud and Sherlock Holmes: Clues and Scientific Method', *History Workshop*, IX, 5–36.

Goodfield-Toulmin, J. (1969) 'Some Aspects of English Physiology, 1780–1840', *Journal of the History of Biology*, II, 283–320.

Granshaw, Lindsay (1985), *St. Mark's Hospital, London: A Social History of a Specialist Hospital*, London: King's Fund Historical Series.

Granshaw, Lindsay (1992) ' "Upon this Principle I have Based a Practice": The Development and Reception of Antisepsis in Britain, 1867–90', in John V. Pickstone (ed.), *Medical Innovations in Historical Perspective*, London: Macmillan, 17–46.

Hamlin, Christopher (1985) 'Providence and Putrefaction: Victorian Sanitarians and the Natural Theology of Health and Disease', *Victorian Studies*, XXVIII, 381–4.

Hamlin, Christopher (1992) 'Predisposing Causes and Public Health in Early Nineteenth-Century Medical Thought', *Social History of Medicine, V, 43–70.*

Hannaway, C. (1981) 'From Private Hygiene to Public Health: A Transformation in Western Medicine in the Eighteenth and Nineteenth Centuries', in Teizo Ogawa (ed.) *Public Health*, Tokyo: Saikon, 108–28.

Heller, Robert (1978) *'Officiers de Santé*: The Second-Class Doctors of Nineteenth-Century France', *Medical History*, XXII, 25–43.

Hilton, Boyd (1988) *The Age of Atonement: The Influence of Evangelicalism on Social and Economic Thought, 1795–1865*, Oxford: Clarendon Press.

Hodgkinson, Ruth (1967) *The Origins of the National Health Service: The Medical Services of the New Poor Law, 1834–1871*, London: The Wellcome Historical Medical Library.

Holloway, S.W.F. (1966) 'The Apothecaries' Act 1815', Part I 'The Origins of the Act', *Medical History*, X, 107–29: Part II 'The Consequences of the Act', *Medical History*, X, 221–36.

Holmes, G. (1982) *Augustan England: Professions, State and Society, 1680–1730*, London: George Allen & Unwin.

Honigsbaum, F. (1979) *The Division in British Medicine: A History of the Separation of General Practice from Hospital Care 1911–1968*, London: Kogan Page.

Honigsbaum, F. (1993) 'Christopher Addison: A Realist in Pursuit of Dreams', in Dorothy Porter and Roy Porter (eds), *Doctors, Politics and Society: Historical Essays*, Amsterdam: Rodopi, 229–47.

Hurst, Sir Arthur (1949) *A Twentieth Century Physician*, London: Edward Arnold & Co.

Ignatieff, Michael (1978) *A Just Measure of Pain: The Penitentiary in the Industrial Revolution, 1750–1850*, London: Macmillan.

Jacyna, L.S. (1983) 'Immanence or Transcendence: Theories of Life and Organization in Britain, 1790–1835', *Isis*, LXXIV, 311–29.

Jacyna, L.S. (1987) 'Medical Science and Moral Science: the Cultural Relations of Physiology in Restoration France', *History of Science*, XXV, 111–46.

Jacyna, L.S. (1988) 'The Laboratory and the Clinic: the Impact of Pathology on Surgical Diagnosis in the Glasgow Western Infirmary, 1875–1920', *Bulletin of the History of Medicine*, LXII, 384–406.

Jacyna, L.S. (1994) *Philosophic Whigs: Medicine, Science, and Citizenship in Edinburgh, 1789–1848*, London: Routledge.

Jewson, N. (1974) 'Medical Knowledge and the Patronage System in Eighteenth-Century England', *Sociology*, VIII, 369–85.

Jewson, N. (1976) 'The Disappearance of the Sick Man from Medical Cosmology, 1770–1870', *Sociology*, X, 225–44.

Jones, Greta (1986) *Social Hygiene in Twentieth-Century Britain*, London: Croom Helm.

Jordanova, Ludmilla (1981) 'Policing Public Health in France 1780–1815', in Teizo Ogawa (ed.) *Public Health*, Tokyo: Saikon, 12–32.

Jordanova, Ludmilla (1989) *Sexual Visions: Images of Gender in Science and Medicine between the Eighteenth and Twentieth Centuries*, New York: Harvester Wheatsheaf.

Keown, John (1988) *Abortion, Doctors and the Law: Some Aspects of the Legal Regulation of Abortion in England from 1803 to 1982*, Cambridge: Cambridge University Press.

Lambert, Royston (1963) *Sir John Simon 1816–1904 and English Social Administration*, London: MacGibbon and Kee.

Larking, Arthur E. 'The General Practitioner and the British Medical Association' *BMJ*, 1907, ii, Supplement 252–4.

Latour, Bruno (1983) 'Give Me a Laboratory and I Will Raise the World', in Karin D. Knorr-Cetina and Michael Mulkay (eds) *Science Observed: Perspectives on the Social Study of Science*, London, Beverly Hills: Sage Publications, 141–69.

Lawrence, Christopher (1975) 'William Buchan: Medicine Laid Open', *Medical History*, XIX, 20–35.

Lawrence, Christopher (1979) 'The Nervous System and Society in the Scottish Enlightenment', in B. Barnes and S. Shapin (eds) *Natural Order: Historical Studies of Scientific Culture*, Beverly Hills: Sage Publications, 19–40.

Lawrence, Christopher (1985a) 'Ornate Physicians and Learned Artisans: Edinburgh Medical Men, 1726–76', in W.F. Bynum and Roy Porter (eds) *William Hunter and the Eighteenth-Century Medical World*, Cambridge: Cambridge University Press, 153–76.

Lawrence, Christopher (1985b) 'Incommunicable Knowledge: Science, Technology and the Clinical Art in Britain, 1850–1914', *Journal of Contemporary History*, XX, 503–20.

Lawrence, Christopher (1988a) 'Alexander Monro Primus and the Edinburgh Manner of Anatomy', *Bulletin of the History of Medicine*, LXII, 193–214.

Lawrence, Christopher (1988b) 'The Edinburgh Medical School and the End of the "Old Thing", 1790–1830', *History of Universities*, VII, 259-86.

Lawrence, Christopher (1992a) 'Democratic, Divine and Heroic: The History and Historiography of Surgery', in C.J. Lawrence (ed.) *Medical Theory, Surgical Practice* London: Routledge, 1–47.

Lawrence, Christopher (1992b) ' "Definite and Material": Coronary Thrombosis and Cardiologists in the 1920s', in Charles E. Rosenberg and Janet Golden (eds) *Framing Disease*, New Jersey: Rutgers University Press, 50–84.

Lawrence, Christopher and Richard Dixey (1992) 'Practising on Principle: Joseph Lister and the Germ Theories of Disease', in C.J. Lawrence (ed.) *Medical Theory, Surgical Practice* London: Routledge, 153–215.

Lawrence, Christopher (1994) 'Disciplining Disease: Scurvy, the Navy, and Imperial Expansion', in D. Miller and P. Reill (eds) *Visions of Empire*, Cambridge: Cambridge University Press.

Lawrence, Susan C. (1988) 'Entrepreneurs and Private Enterprise: The Development of Medical Lecturing in London, 1775–1820', *Bulletin of the History of Medicine*, LXII, 171–92.

Lawrence, Susan C. (1991) 'Private Enterprise and Public Interests: Medical Education and the Apothecaries' Act, 1780–1825', in Roger French and Andrew Wear (eds) *British Medicine in an Age of Reform*, London: Routledge, 45–73.

Lewis, Jane (1992) 'Providers, "Consumers", the State and the Delivery of Health-Care Services in Twentieth-Century Britain', in Andrew Wear (ed.) Medicine in Society, Cambridge: Cambridge University Press, 317–46.

Loudon, I.S.L. (1984) 'The Concept of the Family Doctor', *Bulletin of the History of Medicine*, LVIII, 347–62.

Loudon, I.S.L. (1986) Medical Care and the General Practitioner 1750–1850, Oxford: Clarendon Press.

Lowndes, J. (1956) 'Reminiscences of St. Thomas's', St. Thomas's Hospital Gazette, LIV (December), 194–7.

MacDonald, Michael and Terence R. Murphy (1990) Sleepless Souls: Suicide in Early Modern England, Oxford: Clarendon Press.

McHugh, P. (1980) Prostitution and Victorian Social Reform, London: Croom Helm.

McKendrick, N., J. Brewer and J.H. Plumb (eds) (1982) The Birth of a Consumer Society: The Commercialization of Eighteenth Century England, London: Europa.

McKeown, Thomas (1979) The Role of Medicine: Dream, Mirage or Nemesis?, Oxford: Basil Blackwell.

McLaren, Angus (1993) 'Privileged Communications: Medical Confidentiality in Late Victorian Britain', Medical History, XXXVII, 129–47.

Marcovich, Anne (1982) 'Concerning the Continuity between the Image of Society and the Image of the Human Body: An Examination of the Work of the English Physician J.C. Lettsom (1746–1815)', in Peter Wright and Andrew Treacher (eds), The Problem of Medical Knowledge: Examining the Social Construction of Medicine, Edinburgh: Edinburgh University Press, 69–86.

Marsh, F. 'The Present Position of the Association: the Need of Further Local Organization', BMJ, 1908, i, 1420–3.

Maulitz, Russell C. (1987) Morbid Appearances: The Anatomy of Pathology in the Early Nineteenth Century, Cambridge: Cambridge University Press.

Miley, Ursula and John V. Pickstone (1988) 'Medical Botany around 1850: American Medicine in Industrial Britain', in R. Cooter (ed.) Studies in the History of Alternative Medicine, Basingstoke: Macmillan.

Morgan, Kenneth and Jane Morgan (1980) Portrait of a Progressive: The Political Career of Christopher, Viscount Addison, Oxford: Clarendon Press.

Morris, R.J. (1976) Cholera 1832: The Social Response to an Epidemic, London: Croom Helm.

Mort, Frank (1987) Dangerous Sexualities: Medico-Moral Politics in England since 1830, London: Routledge and Kegan Paul.

Moscucci, Ornella (1990) The Science of Woman: Gynaecology and Gender in England, 1800–1929, Cambridge: Cambridge University Press.

Newman, Sir George (1931) Health and Social Evolution, London: George Allen and Unwin.

Nicolson, M. (1988) 'The Metastatic Theory of Pathogenesis and the Professional Interests of the Eighteenth-Century Physician', Medical History, XXXII, 47–70.

Oppenheim, Janet (1991) ' "Shattered Nerves": Doctors, Patients and Depression in Victorian England, New York: Oxford University Press.

Owen, D. (1965) English Philanthropy 1660–1960, Cambridge, Mass.: Belknap Press.

Park, Katherine (1991) 'Healing the Poor: Hospitals and Medical Assistance in Renaissance Florence', in Jonathan Barry and Colin Jones (eds) Medicine and Charity Before the Welfare State, London: Routledge, 26–45.

Passmore, J.A. (1970) The Perfectibility of Man, London: Duckworth.

Pelling, M. (1978) Cholera, Fever and English Medicine 1825–1865, Oxford, Oxford University Press.

Perkin, Harold (1989) *The Rise of Professional Society: England Since 1880*, London: Routledge.

Peterson, M.J. (1978) *The Medical Profession in Mid-Victorian London*, Berkeley: University of California Press.

Pick, Daniel (1989) *Faces of Degeneration: A European Disorder, c.1848–c.1918*, Cambridge: Cambridge University Press.

Pickstone, John V. (1984) 'Ferriar's Fever to Kay's Cholera: Disease and Social Construction in Cottonopolis', *History of Science*, XXII, 400–19.

Pickstone, John V. (1992) 'Dearth, Dirt and Fever Epidemics: Rewriting the History of British 'Public Health', 1780–1850', in Terence Ranger and Paul Slack (eds) *Epidemics and Ideas: Essays on the Historical Perception of Pestilence*, Cambridge: Cambridge University Press, 125–48.

Porter, Dorothy and Roy Porter (1989) *Patient's Progress: Doctors and Doctoring in Eighteenth-Century England*, Cambridge: Polity Press.

Porter, Dorothy (1991) 'Stratification and its Discontents: Professionalization and Conflict in the British Public Health Service, 1848–1914', in Elizabeth Fee and Roy M. Acheson (eds) A History of Education in Public Health: Health that Mocks the Doctors' Rules, Oxford: Oxford University Press, 83–113.

Porter, R. (1985a) 'William Hunter: A Surgeon and a Gentleman', in W.F. Bynum and R. Porter (eds) *William Hunter and the Eighteenth-Century Medical World*, Cambridge: Cambridge University Press, 7–34.

Porter, R. (1985b) 'Lay Medical Knowledge in the Eighteenth Century: The Evidence of the *Gentleman's Magazine*', *Medical History*, XXIV, 138–68.

Porter, R. (ed.) (1985c) *Patients and Practitioners: Lay Perceptions of Medicine in Pre-Industrial Society*, Cambridge: Cambridge University Press.

Porter, R. (1987) *Mind Forg'd Manacles. A History of Madness from the Restoration to the Regency* London: Athlone.

Porter, R. and Porter, Dorothy (1988) *In Sickness and in Health: The British Experience, 1650–1850*, London: Fourth Estate.

Porter, R. (1989a) *Health for Sale: Quackery in England 1660–1850*, Manchester: Manchester University Press.

Porter, R. (1989b) 'The Gift Relation: Philanthropy and Provincial Hospitals in Eighteenth-Century England', in L. Granshaw and R. Porter (eds) *The Hospital in History*, London: Routledge.

Porter, R. (1991) 'Reforming the Patient in the Age of Reform: Thomas Beddoes and Medical Practice', in Roger French and Andrew Wear (eds) British Medicine in an Age of Reform, London and New York: Routledge, 9–44.

Porter, R. (1992) *Doctor of Society: Thomas Beddoes and the Sick Trade in Late-Enlightenment England*, London: Routledge.

Raistrick, Arthur (1968) *Quakers in Science and Industry*, Newton Abbot: David and Charles.

Rankin, Glynis (1988) 'Professional Organisation and the Development of Medical Knowledge: Two Interpretations of Homeopathy', in R. Cooter (ed.) *Studies in the History of Alternative Medicine*, Basingstoke: Macmillan.

Reiser, S. (1978) *Medicine and the Reign of Technology*, Cambridge: Cambridge University Press.

Richardson, Ruth (1987) *Death, Dissection and the Destitute*, London: Routledge and Kegan Paul.

Rosen, G. (1974) *From Medical Police to Social Medicine: Essays on the History of Health Care*, New York: Science History Publications.

Rosenberg, C. (1979) 'Florence Nightingale on Contagion: The Hospital as Moral Universe', in C. Rosenberg (ed.) *Healing and History: Essays for George Rosen*, Folkestone: Dawson and Sons, 116–36.

Rosenberg, C. (1983) 'Medical Text and Medical Context; Explaining William Buchan's Domestic Medicine', Bulletin of the History of Medicine, LXII, 22–4.

Rosenberg, C. (1987) *The Care of Strangers: The Rise of America's Hospital System*, New York: Basic Books.

Rosner, Lisa (1991) *Medical Education in the Age of Improvement: Edinburgh Students and Apprentices, 1760–1826*, Edinburgh: Edinburgh University Press.

Schiebinger, Londa (1991) 'The Private Life of Plants: Sexual Politics in Carl Linnaeus and Erasmus Darwin', in Marina Benjamin (ed.) Science and Sensibility: Gender and Scientific Enquiry, 1780–1945, Oxford: Basil Blackwell, 121–43.

Scull, Andrew T. (1979) *Museums of Madness: The Social Organization of Insanity in Nineteenth-Century England*, London: Allen Lane.

Shapin, Steven and B. Barnes (1977) 'Science, Nature and Control: Interpreting Mechanics' Institutes', *Social Studies of Science*, VII, 31–74.

Shapin, Steven (1979) 'The Politics of Observation: Cerebral Anatomy and Social Interests in the Edinburgh Phrenology Disputes', in R. Wallis (ed.) *On the Margins of Science: The Social Construction of Rejected Knowledge*, Sociology Review Monograph, XXVII, 139–78.

Slack, Paul (1985) *The Impact of Plague in Tudor and Stuart England*, London: Routledge and Kegan Paul.

Sloan, Philip R. (1990) 'Natural History, 1670–1802', in R.C. Olby, G.N. Cantor, J.R.R. Christie and M.J.S. Hodge (eds) *Companion to the History of Modern Science*, London: Routledge, 295–313.

Smith, F.B. (1979) *The People's Health, 1830–1910*, London: Croom Helm.

Smith, Roger (1992) *Inhibition: History and Meaning in the Sciences of Mind and Brain*, London: Free Association Books.

Spriggs, E.A. (1977) 'John Hutchinson, the Inventor of the Spirometer – His North Country Background, Life in London, and Scientific Achievements', *Medical History*, XXI, 357–64.

Stansfield, Dorothy A. (1984) *Thomas Beddoes M.D. 1760–1808, Chemist, Physician, Democrat*, Dordrecht: Reidel.

Sturdy, Steve (1992a) 'The Political Economy of Scientific Medicine: Science, Education and the Transformation of Medical Practice in Sheffield, 1890–1922', *Medical History*, XXXIV, 125–59.

Sturdy, Steve (1992b) 'From the Trenches to the Hospitals at Home: Physiologists, Clinicians and Oxygen Therapy', in John V. Pickstone (ed.), Medical Innovations in Historical Perspective, London: Macmillan, 104–23.

Taylor, Gordon (1970) 'A Houseman Before World War I', *The London Hospital Gazette*, LXXIII (May), 9–20.

Temkin, O. (1951) 'The Role of Surgery in the Rise of Modern Medical Thought', *Bulletin of the History of Medicine*, XXV, 248–59.

Temkin, O. (1963) 'Basic Science, Medicine and the Romantic Era', *Bulletin of the History of Medicine*, XXXVII, 97–129.

Temkin, O. (1977) 'An Historical Analysis of the Concept of Infection', in *The Double Face of Janus and Other Essays in the History of Medicine*, Baltimore: Johns Hopkins University Press, 456–71.

Thackray, A. (1974) 'Natural Knowledge in Cultural Context: The Manchester Model', *American Historical Review*, LXXIX, 672–709.

Thompson, Paul (1984) *The Edwardians: The Remaking of British Society*, London: Weidenfeld & Nicholson.

Tröhler, Ulrich (1979) 'Quantification in British Medicine and Surgery 1750–1830', University of London, Ph.D. thesis.

Waddington, I. (1973) 'The Role of the Hospital in the Development of Modern Medicine: A Sociological Analysis', *Sociology*, VII, 211–24.

Warner, John Harley (1986) *The Therapeutic Perspective: Medical Practice, Knowledge and Identity in America, 1820–1885*, Cambridge, Mass: Harvard University Press.

Warner, John Harley (1991) 'The Idea of Science in English Medicine: The "Decline of Science" and the Rhetoric of Reform, 1815–45', in Roger French and Andrew Wear (eds) *British Medicine in an Age of Reform*, London: Routledge, 136-64.

Webb, Sidney and Beatrice Webb (1910) *The State and the Doctor*, London: Longmans, Green and Co.

Webster, Charles (1978) 'The Crisis of Hospitals During the Scientific Revolution', in E.G. Forbes (ed.) *Human Implications of Scientific Advance*, Edinburgh: Edinburgh University Press, 214–23.

Webster, Charles (1988) *The Health Services Since the War: Problems of Health Care. Volume I. The National Health Service Before 1957*, London: HMSO.

Webster, Charles (1993) 'The Metamorphosis of Dawson of Penn', in Dorothy Porter and Roy Porter (eds), *Doctors, Politics and Society: Historical Essays*, Amsterdam: Rodopi, 212–28.

Weindling, Paul (1992) 'From Medical Research to Clinical Practice: Serum Therapy for Diphtheria in the 1890s', in John V. Pickstone (ed.), *Medical Innovations in Historical Perspective*, London: Macmillan, 72–83.

Wilson, A. (1985a) 'Participant or Patient? Seventeenth-Century Childbirth from the Mother's Point of View', in R. Porter (ed.) *Patients and Practitioners*, Cambridge: Cambridge University Press, 129–44.

Wilson, A. (1985b) 'William Hunter and the Varieties of Man-Midwifery', in W.F. Bynum and Roy Porter (eds) *William Hunter and the Eighteenth-Century World*, Cambridge: Cambridge University Press, 343–69.

Winter, Alison (1991) 'Ethereal Epidemic: Mesmerism and the Introduction of Inhalation Anaesthesia to Early Victorian London', *Social History of Medicine*, IV, 1–28.

Woodward, J. (1974) *To Do the Sick No Harm. A Study of the British Voluntary Hospital System to 1875*, London and Boston: Routledge & Kegan Paul.

Worboys, Michael (1992a) 'The Sanatorium Treatment for Consumption in Britain, 1890–1914', in John V. Pickstone (ed.), *Medical Innovations in Historical Perspective*, London: Macmillan, 47–71.

Worboys, Michael (1992b) 'Vaccine Therapy and Laboratory Medicine in Edwardian Britain', in John V. Pickstone (ed.), *Medical Innovations in Historical Perspective*, London: Macmillan, 84–103.

Young, R.M. (1990) Mind, Brain and Adaptation in the Nineteenth Century: Cerebral Localization and Its Biological Context from Gall to Ferrier, Oxford: Clarendon Press.

Zihni, Lilian (1989) 'The Relationship between the Theory and Treatment of Down's Syndrome in Britain and America from 1866 to 1967', University of London, Ph.D. thesis.

Index

Abernethy, John, surgeon 35
abortion, attitude of nineteenth-century medical profession 77
accoucheur see midwifery
Addison, Christopher, anatomist and Liberal politician 80, 82
Alison, William Pultney, Edinburgh medical professor 47
Allbutt, Sir Clifford, physician 68
America 5, 17, 37, 55; place in the rise of surgery 64
anaesthesia, place in the rise of surgery 63–4
anatomy 4, 11, 13, 17–20, 28, 34, 38, 59–60; comparative 31, 36; morbid 31; sexual 60
Anatomy Act (1832), significance for medical profession 39–41
antivivisectionism 59–60
apothecaries 3, 9–14, 21, 27; Society of 13–14, 32, 38
Apothecaries Act (1815), origins and significance of 32, 36, 56
Arnott, Neil, sanitary reformer 46
arthritis 11

bacteriology *see* laboratory
barbers *see* surgeons
Barnard, Christiaan, surgeon 1
Beddoes, Thomas, radical physician 28
Bentham, Jeremy 44, 46 *see also* utilitarianism
biology 63, 83; disease as a biological process 3, 75, 86; molecular 1

Black, Joseph, Edinburgh chemistry professor 18
body, the 3, 12, 15, 28, 45; as a biological object 63
British Medical Association (BMA) 77–8, 80
British Medical Journal, The 68–9
Broadbent, W. H., London physician 70
Buchan, William, *Domestic Medicine* 9
Budd, William, Bristol physician 49–50
Butler, Josephine, political campaigner 61

Cambridge 10, 12, 16, 35, 59, 67, 72
Chadwick, Sir Edwin 42–3, 45–9, 61, 64, 80–1; *Report on the Sanitary Condition of the Labouring Population* 43, 47
chemistry 19, 28, 38
childbirth *see* midwifery
cholera 47; epidemics of 41–2, 48–9
Coffin, Albert Isaiah, medical sectarian 37
Coleridge, Samuel Taylor 28
consultants 1, 72, 78–9, 86
consumption 7, 11
Contagious Diseases Acts (1864, 1866), role of medical men 61
Cook, James, voyages of discovery 24–5
Cooper, Sir Astley, surgeon 33
Critchton-Miller, Hugh, psychiatrist 69